I FELT THE CHEERS

THE REMARKABLE SILENT LIFE OF CURTIS PRIDE

Foreword by
Cal Ripken Jr.

I FELT THE CHEERS

THE REMARKABLE SILENT LIFE OF CURTIS PRIDE

Curtis Pride with Doug Ward

KENSINGTON PUBLISHING CORP.
www.kensingtonbooks.com

DAFINA BOOKS are published by

Kensington Publishing Corp.
900 Third Ave.
New York, NY 10022

All Kensington titles, imprints, and distributed lines are available at special quantity discounts for bulk purchases for sales promotions, premiums, fund-raising, and educational or institutional use. Special book excerpts or customized printings can also be created to fit specific needs. For details, write or phone the office of the Kensington special sales manager: Kensington Publishing Corp, 900 Third Ave., New York, NY 10022, Attn: Special Sales Department, Phone: 1-800-221-2647.

Library of Congress Control Number: 2024946452

The DAFINA logo is a trademark of Kensington Publishing Corp.

ISBN: 978-1-4967-5051-8
First Kensington Hardcover Edition: March 2025

ISBN: 978-1-4967-5053-2 (ebook)

10 9 8 7 6 5 4 3 2 1

Printed in the United States of America

To Mom and Dad, who always taught me that anything is possible and never stopped believing in me.

—Curtis Pride

For Heather

—Doug Ward

Contents

Author's Note

Since you are reading this message, I would like to personally thank you for having this book in your hands (or on your electronic device), and your interest in knowing more about my life story.

When I first started succeeding in sports many people would ask me about the specifics of my lack of hearing. Simply put, I have been deaf from the moment I was born. Moreover, since only a miniscule amount of the sound waves entering my ears are ever converted into any sort of actual sound, in medical terminology, I am also considered to be "profoundly deaf."

Since I am deaf, I also fall within the definition of having a "hearing disability." I specifically identify myself as being deaf. But, I do not think of myself as being "handicapped," "disabled," or "hearing impaired." All of those are no longer considered appropriate terminology in our society, and I agree. I have always felt I am "able" to do everything that others can do, except hear. I was pleased when in 2019 Major League Baseball ended their over-100-year use of the term "Disabled List," and instead replaced it with "Injured List" for players who miss games due to an injury.

Additionally, before you begin reading the upcoming chapters, there is another subject I would like to briefly discuss.

Before I was even one year old my parents made the decision to have me try to proceed down the educational path known as oral communication, which is the combination of teaching deaf individuals to read lips and use their voice to speak. Through literally thousands of hours of practice and working with speech therapists,

I gradually improved my lip reading and speech to where it became, for me, a comfortable part of my life.

However, by focusing on the oral approach during my childhood and early adult life, I didn't learn much about American Sign Language (ASL), until after my retirement from playing Major League Baseball when I accepted the job as head baseball coach at Gallaudet University. At that time, I took courses in ASL and, while I am not totally fluent in ASL, I can now have a conversation in ASL in addition to reading lips and speaking orally.

I raise this point because I am familiar with the strong beliefs and opinions that many have regarding oral communication versus ASL. I chose the oral path, but in no way do I have any negative feelings about ASL. For anyone with any degree of hearing loss, I support all methods of communication. It's an individual and personal decision, and a person—and those helping them with that decision— should make whatever choice they think is best.

As you read this book, I hope that you find things that inspire you. It has been a difficult journey for me, filled with many highs— but also quite a few lows— and I felt it was important in the following pages to write about as many of those things as I could.

I also hope this book will inspire everyone with hearing loss to believe that there is nothing to prevent them from still accomplishing all their goals and dreams. Finally, if a parent who gets the same initially shocking diagnosis my parents received—that their child has a hearing disability—can find something in these pages that in any way helps them navigate through the decisions they will then be facing, it will be especially meaningful for me.

Sincerely,
Curtis Pride

Foreword

Curtis and I are both from Maryland and that connection, combined with a mutual love of baseball and basketball, helped us develop a friendship. I knew Curtis had been a standout college point guard at William & Mary, so when I invited him to play in my pick-up basketball games during the off-season, it came as no real surprise that he was one of the best players on the court. Curtis was clearly a great athlete with tremendous focus and drive, but how he played the way he did with a hearing disability amazed me and still does.

During my twenty-one years in the big leagues and growing up around the game, I was fortunate to have very unique experiences. I got to catch the final out in the World Series, play in nineteen All-Star Games, and I was that guy who played in all of those games in a row. But seeing Curtis's improbable dream come true, watching him compete at the game's highest level without the benefit of hearing, was wonderful . . . and hard to fathom. Baseball is a fun game but it's not easy. To succeed, you need to maximize every asset at your disposal. I had no idea how Curtis did it with a hearing disability.

Had I not known Curtis was deaf I never would have guessed it while competing against him in those pick-up basketball games or in big league baseball games because his hearing disability never affected his game. Curtis not only proved he belonged in Major League Baseball, but also elevated every game he played in, demonstrating that anything is possible. And he did it with such grace and selflessness. I remember watching Curtis patiently sign autographs, pose for pictures, and offer words of encouragement and hope to deaf children and their parents before games.

Still, I had unanswered questions. How was a deaf person able to compete with professional athletes without a drop in skill level or a drop off in communication? What was it like to face—and overcome—added obstacles and doubts every time you stepped on a baseball diamond? How did it feel to carry an extra burden every time you walked into a clubhouse or sat down for an interview? How did Curtis make it all look so easy?

On the pages of this book, Curtis takes us inside his silent world to provide the answers. *I Felt the Cheers* is a unique baseball story told by a singular player, one who defied the odds to become the first full season deaf player of the modern era, while also developing into one of baseball's great ambassadors. I am proud to know him.

—*Cal Ripken Jr.*

I FELT THE CHEERS

THE REMARKABLE SILENT LIFE OF CURTIS PRIDE

CHAPTER 1

Destiny's Call

The midnight hour was fast approaching on the night of September 10, 1993, when I settled into my customary spot on the Ottawa Lynx's team bus. It was idling in a desolate parking lot adjacent to a run-down minor-league stadium in Rochester, New York, and I was afraid I would soon be idling into oblivion, too.

My eighth minor-league season was over, which meant my dream of playing in the big leagues was another year closer to ending. I was twenty-four, wrapping up the finest season of my career, and believed I was ready for Major League Baseball. Still, as another year passed by without having received The Call, I couldn't help but wonder if Major League Baseball was ready for me.

I had been playing center field for the Triple-A Lynx and our season had just ended with a 9–3 playoff loss to the Rochester Red Wings. I was preparing to pass the boredom of another overnight bus ride by joining a group of my teammates in one of the card games that convened regularly at the back of the bus.

With players left to their own devices on the back roads and interstates of the International League, most retreated to solitary endeavors. While some watched the movies that were played on TV monitors, the videos were mostly background noise for other activities. Some players read, a few worked crossword puzzles, and some played handheld computer games. Most escaped the tedium of bus travel by sleeping through it.

But I had never been much for isolation. I was born deaf, possibly because my mother was exposed to rubella while she was pregnant with me, although no one knows for sure; and entering the world with a hearing disability presents many unique challenges. I cannot listen to music, and in the darkness of a run-down bus, I can't see well enough to read lips, so I am unable to conduct a simple conversation. It's one of the few times I feel different than everyone else.

I had worked hard to overcome the limits that typically accompany deafness, so I wasn't about to curl up with a good book and I damn sure wasn't going to sleep my way through my baseball career. Poker offered camaraderie and the cards could do my talking, so I almost always joined in. It eased the monotony of the road and helped pass the time, but what I really liked about the games was the give-and-take with teammates. I always found the good-natured competition brought me closer to the other guys and made me feel like I was in the company of comrades rather than riding among strangers commuting on a city bus. It also made me feel like I was no different than my teammates, and at that point in time, there was nothing more important to me.

After eight years in the minors, I had long since figured out that the games on the bus were almost as important as the ones on the field when it came to creating a bond with my teammates. The guys I played cards with always seemed to have a better understanding and acceptance of me. That's what I liked the most about it.

On this night the bus was just minutes from pulling away from the darkened stadium and rolling onto the eastbound lanes of Interstate-90 for what figured to be a subdued 275-mile journey back to Ottawa. There we would clean out our lockers and then go our separate ways. Everyone was ready for the season to be over.

But as I swept up the cards from a folding tray table and looked at my hand, a teammate boarded the bus, poked his head into the game, and dealt me a wild card.

"Curtis Pride," my teammate said, leaning in close enough for me to read his lips in the darkened bus, "Mike Quade wants to see you in the visiting manager's office."

Quade was the Lynx's manager, and right away everyone within earshot knew what this might mean. I knew, too. The Lynx's season was over, but their parent club, the Montreal Expos, was in the thick of a pennant race and figured to be in need of reinforcements. The call to Quade's office might be The Call that every minor-league player lives for, the one I had spent my entire life up to that point dreaming about.

Still, I had my own interpretation of the message: It could be just another of the practical jokes that were so common among minor-league teammates. Sometimes the mischief was good-natured, sometimes not. Once, while I was playing Rookie Ball, my roommate chased me out of our motel room with a knife because I had refused to give the place up for him and a local groupie.

There were plenty of reasons for me to believe this might be just a gag. For as long as I had been playing baseball, many people had held the belief that I didn't have what it takes to make it to the big leagues, that I had too many obstacles to overcome, and I needed to manage my expectations and dreams. A deaf player couldn't possibly communicate well enough in the outfield. He would be uncoachable and could create communication problems inside the clubhouse.

Those stereotypes cut into my confidence, even if I knew deep down they weren't true. The whole thing about getting a jump off the crack of the bat is overrated. In a packed stadium, with the crowd roaring, none of the outfielders can hear it, anyway. If you study physics and sound, you know that sound travels relatively slowly, so the ball leaves the surface of the bat well before the crack of the bat can be heard. The ball is already in flight by the time anyone in the outfield hears any sound.

In truth, I always felt I had an advantage over outfielders who can hear, but I was the only one who believed that to be true. Because I watched only for the ball to leave the bat and didn't listen for the sound of it, I felt I actually got a better jump on fly balls. In that regard I think my deafness worked in my favor. But when the old-school baseball people talk about the crack of the bat, they aren't applying physics to it, and the theory gets repeated so often that it becomes the gospel.

No matter how well I performed, it wasn't uncommon for people to laugh at me behind my back. When I spoke of my dreams for a big-league baseball career, I was told, time and again, that the bigger I dreamed, the bigger my disappointment would be, and that merely playing the game in the minor leagues ought to be enough for me.

Once, I was pelted with hot dogs by fans in the outfield bleachers because they were upset that I didn't respond to their taunting. Another time, when I did respond, fans mocked my deafness, pretending they could not hear me. Sometimes it seemed like I was in a no-win situation.

Then there were the people who treated me like they were doing me a favor by allowing me to be a part of mainstream society. But I wanted the same thing everyone wants—to achieve the highest level of success in my chosen career. And I wanted it to be on merit. So I held my cards close to my chest and braced myself for the punch line. But the messenger just shook his head. No joke. That's when I realized this was real.

I had begun the season at Double-A Harrisburg before being promoted to Triple-A Ottawa and had been playing the best baseball of my life. I was hitting .302 for the Lynx, so I knew there was a chance I might actually be getting called up to Montreal. Yes, deep inside, I was thinking this could be my time, that I might walk into an office and receive the ultimate validation that my deafness was no handicap at all. I already knew that, but still, I wanted this badly. I wanted to be the first deaf player to reach the majors since Dick Sipek in 1945, and the first to play a full big-league season in the modern era—mostly for myself, my parents, and everyone who had helped me along the way. There was also part of me that wanted it so I could prove wrong the people who had doubted me. My parents, John and Sallie Pride, sent me out into the world believing I could accomplish anything, but there were times when it was the people who told me I would never amount to anything that kept me going.

I didn't want to get my hopes up, but our season was over, so what the heck else could it be? Everyone else wondered the same thing. Forty-eight eyes, belonging to twenty-four teammates, focused on me as I walked off the bus. When those teammates began serenading me with a chorus of *oohs* and *aahs,* I grew more anxious. I have always believed my memory is sharper because of my deafness, and even though it was many years ago, I still remember every step I took during that walk between the bus and Mike's office.

The revival that would phase out aging, dilapidated stadiums in favor of modern, retro-style minor-league ballparks was just beginning and had not yet made its way to Rochester, so I made my way through a decrepit clubhouse that was as dingy as it was deserted. Beneath the exposed plumbing and rusty ductwork, which was held together in places with gray tape, the floors were still littered with damp towels and crumpled paper cups.

When I reached a darkened corner of the tiny clubhouse, I spotted the thirty-six-year-old Mike Quade sitting behind a barren desk in a very small dimly lit office, where he was finishing up a call on a clunky black rotary telephone. With my stomach turning, I was eager to learn my fate, so as I stood in a rickety doorway that was encased with layer upon layer of chipped paint, I observed Mike's half of the conversation by reading his lips. Being able to read lips and having excellent vision would be great attributes for a spy, but I make it a point not to eavesdrop on people. Still, this was too important, and I couldn't stop myself from reading Mike's lips.

"Yeah," I could make out Mike saying, "I'll tell him. Okay, I'll make sure he knows. Okay."

The more Mike talked, the more I allowed myself to believe this might be my moment, the one I had dreamed about ever since

I began playing T-ball at the age of six on the baseball fields in suburban Maryland. Mike then hung up the telephone, looked across his desk, and calmly uttered eight simple words most people doubted that I would ever hear: "Congratulations, you're going up to the big leagues."

Of course, I didn't hear them. But I could still see his lips forming the words. "You're going *up* to the big leagues." Mike knew something, all right, because as soon as the words left his lips, my spirits soared. I was on a high. There are feelings I can only get on a baseball field—squaring a ball up on the sweet spot, running down a fly ball on the warning track when everyone in the stadium is sure it's a gapper, and sliding into second or third base, then popping up quickly, spotting an errant throw and taking an extra base. Those were the moments I played for, and they were always better than the paychecks and the adulation combined.

But this moment topped them all and I was standing in a ramshackle office when it happened. Mike was right. I was on the way up. Although I had always told myself that I would remain the same, no matter where my baseball career took me, the world around me was about to change overnight.

"That office was awful," Mike told me years later. "It felt like I was telling somebody in a very cluttered closet that he was going to paradise."

Delivering the news that a player was going to the big leagues was the best part of a Triple-A manager's job, and Mike had done it many times before. While managing in the Expos system, he had already given the word to several players, but he believed I was different.

He told me he liked the fact that I had a level of confidence in my ability that never allowed him to think that I had any doubts. That was not coincidental to the fact that he had shown me so much faith. The more trust a manager shows a player, the easier it is to deliver.

I always felt like I had two opposite forces driving me: the believers and the nonbelievers. Half would lift me up and the other half would drive me down, as if there were equal parts of me riding on both ends of a teeter-totter. The back-and-forth, up-and-down nature of my career was exhausting. It was only after I figured out how to balance the good with the bad, effectively riding in the middle of the seesaw, that I found success.

Mike told me that a minor-league manager can never be sure how a player will react to the news that he had waited his entire life to hear. Some of the players he sent to the majors broke down and cried like babies, right in front of him, right in his office, without shame. Others sat in stunned disbelief that suggested somewhere, deep down inside, they thought themselves unworthy.

I reacted with awe, so Mike did most of the talking. "You belong in the major leagues," he told me. Mike sensed a quality in me that he couldn't quite put his finger on, something he'd never seen before in any other player. The good players always had good instincts, but Mike told me mine were exceptional and I did things he couldn't quite figure out. I was flattered and it meant a lot to me because I had always believed my instincts were my greatest asset. I really felt like Mike understood me, and I was going to miss playing for him.

The instincts he was talking about are a gift. I'm fortunate in that I was blessed with really good senses. My vision is excellent, and I have a keen sense of smell and touch. I have always had a great sense of anticipation and those things have given me an excellent feel for the game.

Triple-A managers double as third-base coaches, and one of Mike's jobs in that capacity was to make sure a base runner didn't get picked off second base. When a runner takes his lead off second, he watches the pitcher and the play in front of him, making it difficult to see if the second baseman or shortstop is creeping in behind him on a pickoff play. When that happens for hearing players, the base coach will simply yell the word "back" to alert the runner. For me, Mike developed a hand signal that he would quickly flash from the third-base coaching box if he saw a middle infielder sneaking in. But many times, that wasn't even necessary.

"I don't know how you did it," Mike once told me, shaking his head in disbelief, "but you were always a step ahead of my arm."

I had my ways. One of them was watching the ground for the opposing player's shadow. If I saw the shadow creeping in, I could quickly scramble back to second base, as if I had eyes in the back of my head.

On a city street I notice reflections in windows because I want to know what's going on around me. I want to make sure no one is sneaking up on me. I had to develop other senses because I lost one. I always must pay attention, just to have a conversation, so I am trained to be attentive at all times and that focus helps me.

During some of my bleakest times, when teammates, fans, or coaches cast doubts on me, one thing kept me going. Deep down I knew something nobody else knew. I felt that not only was my deafness no disadvantage, I believed it could sometimes actually give me an advantage, as it forced me to use senses that players who can hear take for granted.

I noticed everything. And I mean *everything.* In addition to watching for shadows, I would pick up the reflections in shiny batting helmets or other players' sunglasses. If someone wore jewelry, and a lot of players did, I would notice the glint of the gold or a diamond reflecting off the sun or the stadium lights.

And because I was deaf, I could not multitask. When a coach gave me instructions, I focused intently. When I studied what the scouts were saying about opposing pitchers, those reports had my full attention; I was unable to be distracted by music, television, or empty chatter.

Those are the instincts that Mike couldn't put his finger on. Back in his tiny office in Rochester, he reached his arm out to me, shook my hand, and told me to get back on the bus and ride back to Ottawa with the team. The Expos had a 1:00 p.m. game at home the next day against the Cincinnati Reds and they wanted me to be in uniform and ready to play, if needed. After the Lynx team bus arrived back in Ottawa, I was to pack all my clothes and other belongings and drive my own car the remaining 113 miles to Montreal.

When I got back on the bus, I didn't say a word, but the rest of the Lynx players caught the vibe I was sending. It was obvious because of the wide smile that was spread across my face: The Lynx's season was over, but mine was just beginning.

News that a teammate's dream was coming true is not always met with universal approval in minor-league baseball. In football and basketball, a significant percentage of drafted players eventually make it to the top level of those sports. But in baseball, less than one in ten (about 8 percent) of drafted players ever make it to the major leagues, and resentment, jealousy, and the creeping realization that the cost of a teammate's dream coming true might be the death of one's own can have a way of tempering excitement.

However, I sensed no such animosity on the Lynx team bus that night. By relying on the development of homegrown talent, the small-market Expos had cultivated an esprit de corps that pulsed through the organization, and we were an extremely close bunch. When word spread that I had gotten The Call, I could tell that my teammates were genuinely happy for me.

Whenever I joined a new team, the first challenge for me was fitting in with teammates. It wasn't the biggest hurdle for me to clear, but it was always the first, and it was a huge relief to make friends. I walked down the center aisle of the bus, passing through a gauntlet of high fives, and retook my place in the card game. Only, my hands were trembling so badly that I could scarcely make out the cards I held.

My excitement was rivaled only by my fear of the unknown. The bus rides were usually long, especially after a big loss, but this one flew by. The adrenaline coursing through my body prevented me from sleeping, so as the bus crossed the Thousand Islands Bridge, leaving the United States and entering Canada over the St. Lawrence River, I stayed awake, imagining what the next day would be like.

When I tried to sleep, I grew more restless. My mind kept wandering. I looked out the window, but because it was so dark outside, I didn't see the Canadian countryside. Instead, I saw my own reflection in the window. In my mind's eye I didn't see the grown man who was about to make his big-league debut. Instead, I saw the six-year-old version of myself standing at home plate with an oversized hearing aid strapped to my chest, petrified as I played organized baseball for the first time on a dilapidated Little League field, and I thought back to how it all began.

CHAPTER 2

Sound Decisions

My parents have told me they felt I would be an excellent athlete from a very early age. I was an overactive, alert, curious baby. According to my mother, before I was a year old, I was already crawling around the house. At around one year old, I could spring out of my crib, slide down the rails, and off I would go.

It was my mother who first became concerned about my hearing. Back then, unlike today, there weren't any screening tests for hearing that could be performed on babies shortly after birth. I was my parents' second child, and while I was very active, within months after I was born, my mother could sense something might be wrong when I didn't respond to simple verbal cues, or toys that would make noise, the way my older sister, Jacqui, had at similar points in her development.

My mom realized that everything I did was vision based and that I only responded to visual stimulus. I was a sound sleeper, undisturbed by dogs barking, doors slamming, or people talking near my crib.

"You didn't even want to bang pots and pans," my mom told me. "Every kid wants to do that."

After an audiologist conducted an audiogram, the results documented my profound sensorineural hearing loss and that's when my mom and dad began to do a lot of research. They both agreed that I would be best served by one of them staying at home, making my well-being a primary focus. They knew they couldn't just hire a babysitter and expect her to do the things necessary to both take care of me and ensure my development. My mom volunteered for the assignment, giving up her career as a registered nurse to stay home and devote her full-time attention to my development.

My diagnosis was that I had been born with profound sensorineural deafness. Basically, in sensorineural deafness, there is damage to the auditory nerves that convert the vibration and sound waves entering the ear to sound and words as those signals are transferred to the brain. My degree of sensorineural deafness was diagnosed as "profound," which means that only a very small portion of the sound waves and vibrations that enter my ears are converted to any form of "sound" by my auditory nerves.

As various audiologists did more detailed tests on me when I was two years old, they recommended to my parents that I wear a small rectangular external hearing device on my chest. A few years later, audiologists advised me to switch to a hearing aid in my left ear, which would slightly amplify the sound vibrations entering that ear. I have continually worn a hearing aid in my left ear since I was about seven years old, all throughout my entire professional baseball career, and continuing to the present time. The hearing aid doesn't convert sound into understandable words, but it does allow me to detect various noises that may be occurring around me.

My parents also had to decide how I would learn to communicate. They spent countless hours meeting with audiologists and were told about three options: oral communication, Cued Speech, or American Sign Language (ASL).

Oral communication meant learning to read lips, learning to pronounce words, and developing my voice, and was by far the most difficult option. Cued Speech had been developed by Dr. R. Orrin Cornett in the mid-1960s and was considered cutting-edge when I was born in 1968. At its core Cued Speech believes all language communication is based in mastering the phonemic base of spoken languages. By combining mouth movements with hand gestures, words and sentences can be built. The system is versatile and can be used for virtually any language.

The third option, American Sign Language, is the most common form of communication in the Deaf community. As the name implies, it involves learning a hand sign that correlates to a word or phrase. The signs are largely intuitive—the sign to indicate smell, for instance, involves fanning your hand in front of your nose—and the system is quite ingenious.

My father traveled a lot for his job, and wherever he went, he would make it a priority, on his own time, to visit a deaf school in the city where he was working. The more research he did, the more success stories he found regarding oral communication.

After all their research and guidance from professionals in deaf education, my parents opted for the oral approach. They felt it would present the best option for me to develop to my maximum potential. And, in retrospect, the choices my parents made turned out to be great for me.

The next thing my parents had to do was decipher where I would have the best chance of developing into someone who could speak proficiently. At around the time of my first birthday, they enrolled me part-time in the oral education component program at Children's Hospital in Washington, DC, and I received quality services through the part-time program there for two years. Shortly before my third birthday, the program at Children's Hospital recommended that I attend full-time.

My father has often told me about a saying his father taught him: "It's better to be born lucky than rich." As it turns out, this was very true regarding my education. My parents learned that right across the Washington, DC, city line, the Montgomery County, Maryland, Public School System was operating one of the best and most comprehensive deaf education programs in the United States. At that time it was the only school system in the country that gave parents a choice of all the various program options: total communication, oral, sign language, and Cued Speech.

After they had studied all the data, moving to Montgomery County and suburban Silver Spring, Maryland, was the best alternative for our family. It meant I could be enrolled in one of the best educational programs for deaf children in the entire country; Jacqui could receive a top-rate public education; and my father could continue to commute to his government job and maintain his position at the Department of Health and Human Services in downtown Washington. So we moved to Montgomery County in 1971, and I was enrolled in the oral preschool program there.

For support my mother and father joined the Montgomery County Association for Hearing-Impaired Children, and it turned out to be an excellent decision. They met other parents who had older and younger deaf children and found it to be a wonderful opportunity to share information and learn from others.

The association had guest speakers, bringing in national experts like Dr. Winifred Northcott, who was a pioneer in emphasizing oral education for deaf kids in Minnesota. They had monthly meetings and fundraisers and purchased books for their library on hearing disability and deafness. It was all extremely helpful for parents whose children were enrolled there to provide feedback that they were on the right track.

We would be evaluated every six months, and sometimes my response to the challenges I faced would be misinterpreted as behavioral issues. I remember going through a period of obsessively playing with a pencil, sometimes drumming it on my desk, sometimes twirling it between my fingers like a miniature baton, all without realizing I was doing so. It was a normal response to the challenges I was facing, but my speech therapists and teachers would monitor me a little more closely. My deafness would not allow for daydreaming or multitasking. I had to watch and focus on my teachers, fully and completely, always. Concentrating nonstop could be exhausting.

Becoming oral was never a smooth and easy path, but rather one full of twists and turns. Sometimes a child's mother and father have different views on what is best for their child, and that can lead to conflict at home. My father told me whenever he would grow impatient with my progress, frustrated at what I was going through, my mother—the former nurse gifted with uncommon patience and strong nurturing instincts, which are essential to good nurses—would give him a kick in the rear and explain to him that it would not be easy, but in the long run, the payoff would be well worth the added challenges.

My father had the added weight of straddling two worlds. He would return from a business trip, where he had operated at a high-speed tempo, conducting interviews, leading meetings, and traveling from city to city at a breakneck pace. Then he would come home, where everything in our household functioned on a different level to accommodate for my deafness. It would take some time for him to get reacquainted with the world of a deaf child and the whole world my family had created to make me feel normal, which also allowed for my development.

My mother, meanwhile, had to take care of Jacqui, who had her own needs. My parents never made me feel like I was a burden, but when I look back, my deafness certainly complicated their world. Jacqui was always in a program for gifted students, which meant she had a lot more activities and homework assignments to do. It would have been impossible for my mother to tend to the different needs of Jacqui and me if she had kept working as a nurse. I am lucky she made the choice she did.

There was a fine line between being a teacher and parent, and my folks had to find the proper balance and remember that they were my parents, first and foremost. Dr. Northcott, the influential therapist from Minnesota, tells a story about a girl whose mother would correct her every time she said something that did not come out of her mouth sounding like perfect English.

The girl grew frustrated with her mother. "You don't care what I say," the girl said, "you only care how I say it." My father says it was a powerful story that served as a reminder to him and other parents that being a parent was more important than being a surrogate speech therapist.

While I didn't learn sign language as a child, I believe we all use an intuitive kind of physical language to communicate when necessary. And I have since learned sign language during my adult years, and I think it is a terrific addition to my overall ability to communicate with everyone.

On the concept of using physical language to communicate, I remember one night, when I was about five, our family had gone out to eat at a fast-food restaurant, and my mom asked me to go get straws from the man behind the counter. Only I hadn't learned to correctly say the word "straws" and it kept coming out like "twalls." The poor man working the counter had no idea, until I finally pursed my lips and pantomimed sucking through an imaginary straw. Presto, I got straws. It made me wonder if it wouldn't be easier to instinctively play out every word as if I were in one giant game of charades.

During my entire childhood, when I would come home from school, I would do my homework with my mom, and we would practice all types of sounds and words. My mom developed a system of pictures to deal with abstract concepts. As hard as I have worked, and as much as I've learned, there are nuances I understand in theory but cannot pick up on in everyday life because they are based in tone or inflection. Things like sarcasm, double entendres, and bad puns all fly over my head. My mom never wanted me to look like I was an oddball, who didn't fit in, so she once told me that if I didn't understand a story or a joke that everyone else was laughing at, just laugh right along with everybody.

I found this to be especially true when I was watching TV with a group of people. I would often just join in with the crowd when they would laugh. Then, about the time I was in middle school, came one of the greatest advancements of this deaf man's life. Closed captioning was made available on most American television programming, and now when I laugh, it is genuine. Even more satisfying were the times I was able to pick up on a subtle joke, usually the kind that deals with a movie's plot or a particular character's personality. Because I am forced to follow along so closely when I am watching television, I am sometimes able to see something a person only mildly engaged might miss.

I used a telecommunications device for the Deaf—commonly referred to as a TTY machine (teletypewriter)—to make phone calls. The TTY, which enabled a deaf person to have a phone conversation with a hearing person, became essential for me when I left home to play minor-league baseball and, subsequently, attend college.

The TTY machine looked a lot like a small electric typewriter, with a coupler on top for the telephone's receiver. Above the keyboard there was a small screen, which would display the typed text message in a rolling LCD readout screen that looked a lot like the scroll across the bottom of a television screen. My parents always felt that receiving news from me via words scrolling across their TTY in lights made even the most mundane update seem like important breaking news, as if they were watching it on the ticker in New York's Times Square.

The TTY was a precursor to text messaging, and today I still marvel that a large faction of the hearing world now prefers communicating via text messaging. After years of working to build a bridge to the hearing world, I get a kick out of the fact that the hearing world has now crossed over into my territory.

Still, not even modern technology can eliminate all the challenges a deaf person must deal with. Several years ago I boarded a Metro train in Washington, DC, headed for my parents' house in suburban Maryland. I was bound for the Glenmont Station, located near my parents' place, but I was tired and fell asleep. Unable to hear the conductor announce the train would be put out of service after the Forest Glen Station, and all riders were required to exit and board a replacement train, I slept uninterrupted while everyone collected their belongings and disembarked at the Forest Glen Station, two stops away from my destination.

I continued to slumber on the Metro—now out of service and essentially a ghost train—until I woke up in total darkness on the out-of-service train, unaware of my surroundings and completely baffled by what had happened. Where was I? It felt like the Twilight Zone.

Ultimately, a conductor executing his nightly walk-through found me and explained that I was on a train in the yard near the Forest Glen Station. When I told him that because of my deafness, I had not heard the announcement to depart the train at the Forest Glen Station, he was sympathetic to my situation and helpful.

The conductor had to pull the train out of the yard and back onto the mainline track and drive the train back to the Forest Glen Station, where he dropped me off and I waited for the next train to take me to the Glenmont Station. There, I met my mother, who had come to the station to pick me up.

My parents weren't the only people who put my well-being ahead of their own. Randy Hurowitz was a good friend of our family and lived nearby and would always make sure I was involved in anything that was going on. Randy's sister had a hearing disability and he understood what it took to keep a person with a hearing disability engaged.

My sister Jacqui was always great, too. One time we were at the lake swimming, and I went out on the pier and there were fish around. One guy thought I had a cognitive disability—he kept telling me to jump in and grab a fish, but I knew better, and Jacqui stood up for me. Jacqui and I had different interests and our own separate lives much of the time, but when we were together, we shared the kind of strong bond only siblings can know.

I was always a big dreamer and set big goals for myself. My academic achievements and athletic success all started there, but if my parents had not believed in me and my dreams, it would have all ended there. It came as no surprise to them that when I got older, I tried every sport imaginable: baseball, swimming, gymnastics, track, flag football, tennis. You name it—I tried it. With one exception there wasn't a sport I wasn't involved in. The only sport I never attempted was tackle football, because my folks wouldn't let me play it. They were way ahead of the times in their awareness of the risk of concussions and other severe injuries in football.

I didn't realize it at the time, of course, but I was very fortunate to grow up in a household with two strong role models for parents, and two smart, ambitious sisters. My sister Jacqui is two years older than me, and my sister Christine is eight years younger. They say you are whom you associate with, and my family gave me a huge head start on achieving my dreams.

Every decision my parents made was always in my best interest and helped to reinforce my belief in myself. Had they taken the easy way out and kept me protected from hardship and heartache, my life would have been easier, but nowhere near as fulfilling. Just as striking out or making an error is a part of baseball, disappointment and failure are a part of life. My parents were wise enough to realize that those challenges, and my experiencing some of life's inevitable disappointments, would in the long run make me stronger.

CHAPTER 3

Little League, Big Dreams

To this day, I believe the biggest at bat of my life came when I was six years old. It was my first T-ball game, and I wore a deck of card–sized hearing aid, tucked in a pouch my mom made, harnessed to my chest. There were wires running down the device, attaching to a custom mold that fit behind my ear.

I felt like an old car that was being jump-started, and the long wire that protruded from my shirt and into my left ear made me look like a robot that was being restrained by electrical cables in some low-budget horror movie. When I ran, the device would bounce up and down, and I was in constant fear of it breaking loose, smashing into a million little pieces as it hit the ground. But mostly I was afraid of how it made me look and what other kids would think of me.

This was 1974, and in those days political correctness had not yet made its way into popular culture. Neither had common human decency. It wasn't unusual for kids— both teammates and opponents—to make fun of me because of the hearing aid and the way I talked with a speech impediment. It was also common for a deaf person to be perceived as being slow or having mental issues.

Nothing did more damage to the deaf community, and to me personally, than the alliteration "deaf and dumb." The term insidiously made people think that being hearing impaired was synonymous with being stupid. The irony, of course, is that the original definition of the word "dumb" in that phrase is *unable to speak*. Later, the definition of "dumb" was revised to include *lacking intelligence*.

The first thing I can remember wanting was to be a baseball player, and those stereotypes about deafness threatened to end my baseball career before it started. My parents had signed me up to play in a league sponsored by the Wheaton, Maryland, Boys Club. I was extremely excited about getting the chance to play baseball. Soon after, my dad and I went to the local sporting-goods store, where I picked out a glove. But while I was breaking that glove in, there existed the possibility I would miss out. When the coaches and administrators met to allocate players to teams in a modified draft, one name was conspicuously absent and unavailable—mine.

The league's administrators were convinced I had no place in the league, that my presence would be a burden to everyone involved, although they didn't put it that way. The excuse they used was age, although there were concrete examples of exceptions to the age requirement. When my father was informed of their decision, he politely told league officials that his son would, in fact, be playing. He told them they could do it the easy way, or the hard way, which would have entailed legal proceedings. My father was not bluffing. When he says something, he has invariably thought about the long-term implications and is prepared to act on them. Had the league not rescinded their decision, he was prepared to lawyer up.

Instead, the league reached out to a wonderful man named Don Stein, the coach they believed was most likely to accept me on his team. "We have a lost cause. A player with two strikes against him: He is deaf, and he is Black. His father is making a fuss, so somebody has got to take him. Will you do it?"

If it takes a village to raise a child, it takes a planet to get a deaf kid from the suburbs of Washington, DC, all the way to the big leagues; and, outside of my own family, Don Stein was the first person in the universe of sports to offer me hope and encouragement. Not only did Don take me on his team, but he was also incredibly open-minded and patient, taking time to work with my father and me.

It wasn't so much that Don made me a better player, which he did, but it was more a case of him allowing me to *believe* I could be a good player. If there is one thing my deafness has taught me, it's that we make our own luck, and that perseverance and hard work are just as important, if not more important than talent. Had Don not taken me on his team, I would have taken another path, and I believe I still would have eventually been successful. But that road would have been longer, bumpier, and there were no guarantees.

Don was the first person outside of my family to open a major door for me and, in doing so, he began a butterfly effect that altered my life's course for the better, and I will always be eternally grateful. By my second year of playing for Don, his tutelage helped me become the team's first baseman and leading hitter. Don wasn't the only one who believed in me. While my teammates were skeptical and dismissive at first, my ability to hit soon won them over and I became accepted as a teammate.

It's funny, in Don, the league had the perfect solution to what they deemed a problem—me—but didn't even consider it until my father forced their hand. My parents shielded me from the story until I was a teenager, but when they finally told me, it came with a couple of valuable lessons: Don't take no for an answer, and you must be an active participant in your own rescue. While the Wheaton Boys Club no longer exists, I don't have any ill will toward the administrators. After the rocky start my participation was an overwhelming positive experience. They could have broken me, but, thanks to my father and Don Stein, they gave me a great gift that I have carried with me throughout my life.

Little League Baseball was the first party I crashed without an invitation, but it wouldn't be the last. Often I feel like the guy at the door, desperately trying to talk my way past the bouncer.

My parents, meanwhile, wanted desperately to open every door for me. They were active in the local association for the deaf, which was a strong advocate of oral communication. The University of Maryland is just twenty-five miles from my hometown, and my parents watched, firsthand, as Steven Rattner, whose hearing loss was similar to mine, became the first deaf person to graduate from the University of Maryland's School of Dentistry. Steven was oral, and his ability to find success in the academic world was an enormous inspiration to me. He also helped to convince my parents that oral communication could provide the greatest number of options for me later in life.

The next big decision would come from me: After the sixth grade I convinced my parents to allow me to attend my neighborhood middle school, instead of a middle school in a different area of the county that offered special services for the deaf. I would like to say that my choice was based on an undying self-confidence and a desire to achieve at the highest possible level, but that would be a lie. The fact of the matter is that I wanted to go to the same school as my sister Jacqui, and I just wanted to be seen as a normal kid in the neighborhood. The middle school was less than a mile from our house; and to me, it seemed like a waste of time to be bussed across town to a school with more deaf kids.

My decision was met with great skepticism from the audiologists and deaf educators with whom we had been working. They believed I was setting myself up for failure—something that could set me back years—because the mainstream schools had limited accommodations for a deaf student. While the experts in the Deaf community were urging my parents to send me to a school for the deaf, we found an ally in Argyle Middle School principal Lewis Jones. When my parents took me to meet with Mr. Jones, I was adamant about attending a mainstream school, but my folks were still unsure. After all, they wanted what was best for me, and if that meant riding a bus for thirty minutes each way to attend a school that had more help available, that's what I would do.

Lewis Jones, however, had other ideas. He was a hands-on principal, a man who took great pride in being involved in all aspects of his school. He was also a man willing to take on a challenge, and, let's face it, at that point in my life, I was nothing if not challenging. He assured my parents that if I attended Argyle, it would be a positive experience and he would look out for me as if I were his own son.

With that, Lewis cast the deciding vote, and I entered the world of mainstream education. If we are lucky, we all have people who believe in us when no one else does—people who make a difference in our lives. Lewis Jones joined Don Stein on the list of people who helped keep my life on track, heading in the right direction, when the slightest detour could have changed my course forever.

Getting into Argyle Middle School was the easy part. Getting through it was another thing altogether. I was excited to be joining Jacqui and walking to a school near our house, but deep down I was terrified. It was a classic case of "be careful what you wish for because you just might get it." I got my wish and now I had to work to keep it.

Other than Jacqui, I only knew a couple of other kids in the school, and I was both shy and self-conscious about my deafness. Argyle Middle School could just as well have been Harvard; I had no idea how I would stack up in the classroom. What I had more than anything was doubt. I had an oral interpreter for some of my classes, a setup I wasn't crazy about because I just wanted to be like everyone else; but for the more difficult subjects, it was necessary.

I was lucky to have Jacqui. She could have felt like I was a burden, or I was crowding her space, but she went out of her way to introduce me to her friends. Though I hardly had any friends at Argyle, some of the kids there had seen my early exploits on the athletic fields and were welcoming because they believed I could be an asset. I was thrilled that my athletic talent preceded me, but at that point I was more thrilled just to find any level of acceptance.

When I was back in elementary school, not everyone welcomed me with open arms. I was always the fastest kid in school, and when we would have races during recess, I would always win. This would include outrunning the school bully, who was in sixth grade, and winning the race gave my class home field advantage.

But being frequently outrun by the deaf kid did not sit well with the bully, so he did what bullies do and began kicking me around, making fun of me, and hitting me. It was an emotional roller coaster, coming off the high of winning a footrace, only to be denigrated and beaten up by his fists. I'd go home crying, so my father taught me to defend myself, how to fight.

The next day the bully picked on me as usual, but this time I pushed back. A fight ensued, and when I got the best of the bully, I suddenly had even more credibility with my classmates on the playground. The bully never bothered me again, and I had learned a valuable lesson that I carried with me to middle school.

In seventh grade my athletic ability led to one of the most profound relationships of my life. One day a classmate named Steve Grupe noticed that I was the only student who did not take notes. He had seen me on the baseball field and was impressed with my game. Being very shrewd, Steve saw an opportunity. He offered to share his notes with me on one condition: I help him become a better baseball player.

What began as a mutually beneficial business arrangement developed into much more. Steve and I soon became best friends and remain so to this day. Steve was in the stands when I got my first major-league hit, and he named his son (my godson) after me.

Steve gave me his notes in middle school, and I gave him pointers on how to be a better baseball player, but I still believe I got the better of the deal. In addition to his copious notes on everything from science and math to American history, Steve gave me the belief that I had something to offer, that I had been given a gift I could share with others. I began to sense that being different could frequently be a good thing.

CHAPTER 4

How Did This Happen?

While I was playing in the big leagues, I developed a game day routine that began with a pregame meal consisting of a chicken Caesar salad and an iced tea. I would ritualistically go to a restaurant or diner, then proceed to order the exact same thing, as if I were Popeye downing a can of spinach in one of those old cartoons, the contents of which would be the key to activating my superhuman strength.

When I was playing for the Detroit Tigers, I remember taking a seat in a restaurant for an early lunch before a game that night and engaging in idle conversation with the waitress. We talked about the weather, and I mentioned that I was originally from Maryland, at which time she offered up the various attractions Detroit could offer a visitor. It was standard, folksy small talk that was both benign and welcoming at the same time.

Then she took my order.

"Chicken Caesar salad with iced tea," I said.

When she brought out the tea, she asked if I needed sugar or lemon.

"Sugar," I said.

This was met by a silence so profound, even a deaf person could hear it.

Sometimes the *sh* sound in the letter *S* can trip me up, and the way I pronounced "sugar" must have been awkward, because any rapport we had built dissolved quickly, as if a nuclear bomb had been detonated. It wasn't an explosion, of course, but rather the instant she realized I was deaf, our interaction was different.

Her speech slowed, her countenance drooped with a look of concern as she went over the top to cater to my every need, as if she were a first responder tending to an accident victim on the side of the road. Her reaction was honest and her treatment of me was based on concern, not contempt, but it was not something I wanted or felt I needed.

I also remember what turned out to be a very funny story when I stopped at a fast-food restaurant one afternoon on my way home from college. The young man behind the counter, who looked to be about eighteen years old, was having difficulty understanding my order. I couldn't read his lips very well when he asked me a question, so I asked him to repeat the question while at the same time pointing at my hearing aid and saying, "I'm deaf."

At that point he got very excited, saying, "Wait! Wait! We just had a meeting about this, and I have something in the back office for you!" He then went back through the kitchen, ran back to the counter, and handed me a laminated copy of their menu . . . that was all in Braille!

Although the reaction of the young man at the fast-food restaurant was obviously unusual and he meant well, it is not at all uncommon for people to have some type of reaction when meeting me for the first time. There is often a period when I interact with someone in a restaurant, on an airplane, or at a Starbucks, when I pass for hearing. For a time, usually a few moments, sometimes longer, a server, a flight attendant, or a barista will not realize that I am deaf. Somewhere along the course of our interaction—maybe due to the way I pronounce a certain word, or perhaps because the person I'm talking to spots the hearing aid behind my left ear, it hits them: They are having a conversation with a deaf person. It surprises them and their expression changes in an instant, along with the way they treat me.

For a moment they might try to figure out if I have an accent, or if I'm a little drunk. Sometimes they ask me what country I am from, as if English is my second language. When I tell them that I am deaf, they invariably say, "I'm sorry" or "You speak well for a deaf person." Doing anything well "for a deaf person" was never my intent. It was never acceptable, either. I wanted to do things well.

Full stop.

For the longest time this seismic shift in someone else's perception of me, being proffered the moral victory of speaking well "for a deaf person," angered me. Today I am at a point in my life where I am no longer affected by someone else's reality, only my own.

It's a tricky business, being deaf in a hearing world. I have never tried to portray myself as someone who can hear, nor would I ever try to hide the fact that I cannot. It is mere fact, and it brings neither pride nor shame. It's just who I am. Still, I can't deny that I now get a huge kick out of momentarily passing for someone with the ability to hear. I no longer get upset by the shift in someone's treatment of me when they realize I am deaf. Instead, I see it for what I believe it to be: a resounding vote of approval to all the speech therapists I worked with to help me become efficient at both speech and lip-reading.

My ability to enunciate words I have never heard is the result of years and years of intense speech therapy. I think it is part of the reason I was always able to bring focus and a strong work ethic to my baseball career. Malcolm Gladwell has made famous the notion that you need ten thousand hours in any discipline to become proficient at it, and, in my estimation, I had at least fifty thousand hours of therapy to master the art of speaking. I should be pretty good at it.

Whenever I meet someone new or share my story at a speaking engagement, I always get the same question: How am I able to have conversations with people when I can't hear? The answer comes in two parts. First, I tell them, I learned to speak. Then I learned to read lips by studying the mouth movements for the words I had just learned to pronounce.

That I was able to master those two disciplines is the result of a lot of very smart and dedicated speech therapists. My parents were pivotal, too, in that they made my development a priority. I believe my own determination was the X factor that enabled me to put these two elements together and communicate in the hearing world.

The foundation for my ability to carry on a conversation was established as a three-year-old when I began intensive speech therapy. Every day I would visit a speech therapist, who would take my hand and hold it to her neck, enabling me to feel the vibrations that came as she pronounced every letter in the alphabet. Those individual letters became the building blocks of my vocabulary.

The therapist would then teach me to differentiate between the sounds of each letter when she pronounced it. I was instructed to take note of the way every letter felt different on my hand when she spoke it. Then she would show me a flash card displaying a picture of something—say a chair, or a horse, or a car—with the corresponding word written below.

As I fixated on the flash card with the picture and appropriate letters spelling out the object, my therapist would pronounce the word. My hand, still on her neck, would feel the vibration of the word; somehow my brain would put it all together and I would understand what any given word looked like in print and how it felt on my hand—or how it "sounded."

Learning to communicate all came down to repetition. Learning the sound and feel of a letter, then putting words together when I would feel the speech therapist's neck as she pronounced them. From this, I learned to speak. While I was feeling my therapist's throat, I would watch her lips. It was the sound—and feel—combined with the visual movement of her lips as she enunciated the words. Lip-reading is my first language, learned and developed at an age when most kids are learning to talk. After I had the basics, I was able to develop my lip-reading through years and years of repetition.

The process required great focus, attention to detail, and mostly a whole lot of patience from everyone involved, me included. Maybe it was just determination, as I wanted to prove I was no different. I wanted to prove I was just a normal kid, who wished to be treated like a normal kid. My earliest goals were modest. I didn't want to be patronized, nor did I want to be different.

Deciphering the gray area between therapy and reality didn't always come easily. My parents would act as home tutors, reinforcing what I had learned in therapy. One night my mother held up a set of car keys while saying the word "keys." Then she asked me, "What do you see on my lips?"

Easy, I thought, and blurted out the obvious answer: "Smile!" I was both right and wrong, and after a hearty laugh, my mother patiently explained she didn't mean "on my lips" in the literal sense, but rather "what words are my lips speaking."

I had speech therapy for seventeen years. By the time I was about four or five years old, I could communicate. But I was far from perfect. Despite my hard work, kids would still make fun of the way I talked, mock me, and laugh. It was frustrating because I would spend hours in therapy and kids would still have a laugh at my expense. Many days I would come home angry, crying, and upset. But it just made me more persistent in my desire to speak as well as I could.

Every year I would enhance my vocabulary and polish my ability to enunciate by adding increasingly complex words to my vocabulary. While the hearing aid I wear on my left ear enables me to detect sounds—shoes walking on tile, hands banging on a computer keyboard, vague noises—I cannot make out actual words. The sounds are too complex, my hearing loss too profound for a hearing aid to be of significant help in speech communication.

Through all this repetition I was oral by the time I was in middle school. Because I learned very young, speaking and reading lips were all second nature to me. Just as learning a foreign language comes easier the younger you are, so, too, is youth an advantage for a deaf person trying to learn to speak.

My success in learning to speak at a young age gave me confidence.

Because I had my own way of interacting with others, I began to think maybe I could apply the same principle to baseball and began thinking about unusual ways to play the game.

It was like my personal version of the highly popular baseball book *Moneyball*, and I began to look for underappreciated ways to exploit the game. For example, I soon realized that while I couldn't hear teammates or opponents approaching, I could compensate by watching a shadow with my peripheral vision.

That's when baseball became a game of inches and geometry to me. I would watch the ball, see the angle of it coming off the bat, to judge fly balls. My vision was always very good, so I used a strength to compensate for a weakness. It's a concept that became sort of a mantra for me, in all aspects of my life.

My parents always wanted me to play a variety of sports and that's what I advise kids today. Playing different sports helped me to develop confidence and gave me the opportunity to interact with teammates, and the confidence to develop friendships. Without sports I would have been a shut-in once the final school bell rang and I went home. Sports made me the person I am today. Without them I believe I ultimately would have found success because I am an optimist, but, in all honesty, I have no idea how I would have accomplished it. Sports were also important in the sense it gave other people a chance to interact with me, a chance to learn I'm not so different.

If you wanted to pick the ideal team sport for a deaf person to play, it would not be baseball. It is a game that requires communication between teammates, particularly in the outfield. Basketball, too, requires verbal interaction between teammates, especially on defense. The team sport best suited to a deaf person is probably soccer because it is so spread out. Vision and a feel for the game are more important in soccer than the ability to hear.

None of those factors, however, were taken into consideration when I envisioned how my life would unfold. As a child I had many dreams, and I believed the bigger the dream, the better. I never allowed my deafness to have a vote in what I attempted. I never allowed deafness to have any impact on my life at all. Not on a baseball diamond and not in a restaurant.

The hardest place of all was not allowing it to have an impact inside my own head.

CHAPTER 5

Goal Oriented

Behavioral scientists believe the odds of achieving a goal increase significantly when you write it down. I had no way of knowing this when, as a twelve-year-old, I prepared a written list of fifty goals I wanted to achieve in my lifetime, but I believe when I created that list, I was drawing up a road map for my life.

Today my idea would be called a bucket list, or a master plan, but for a starry-eyed deaf kid in the 1980s, the list I created might just as well have been called the Impossible Dream. Luckily, I was too young to know better, and had too much familial support to rip up the list and toss it in the trash can when that might have been the smartest choice.

The list was a way of challenging myself, just to see what I could achieve. Some of the objectives seemed simple, like breaking the record on the video game *Galaga* at the local ice-cream shop. It might sound juvenile, but I am convinced every goal you reach bolsters your confidence, so they were all important to me.

My video game obsession began when my next-door neighbor and I would go to the local ice-cream parlor, Zipz, every weekend. We'd get a cone and spend the day playing *Galaga, Pac-Man,* and *Donkey Kong.* I'd be there for hours upon hours, dropping up to twenty dollars into the coin slot in a single sitting, refusing to give up until I had a new record.

I started mowing lawns to support my love of video games, and one of my clients, Rick Barsky, became a good friend. Sadly, Rick passed away in February 2023, but he was always a huge sports fan and loved to talk with me about sports and my career in professional baseball. Rick was also a certified public accountant, and while I obviously didn't need financial advice while I was mowing lawns, Rick would later become my accountant. He did an excellent job handling my financial planning and taxes throughout my adult life, and, of course, remained a good friend. Rick's passing from a fast-spreading cancer was sudden and unanticipated and I miss having him as a close friend.

Looking back on my childhood passion for video games, people gave me a hard time about spending every extra quarter that came into my possession on video games, but going after those records taught me a lot about setting goals and the satisfaction that comes with achieving them. When I finally established the high score of over two million, there was an indescribable feeling of accomplishment in typing my initials—*CJP*—into the machine for everyone in Silver Spring to see and envy. I've never craved fame, but I always wanted respect, and that's what being immortalized in the video machine represented to me.

The record didn't last (because they never do), but the lesson did. For a moment, at a certain place and time, I was better than anyone at something, and I had my first taste of the power of achievement. That it came playing a video game in a local ice-cream shop didn't matter. What did matter was that I began to believe in myself in a way that had not happened anywhere but the baseball diamond.

When I went home that night, I pulled the list from under my bed and placed a huge check mark next to the video game goal on my list and again felt the tingle of achievement. As I crawled into bed, I began to wonder: *If I can master* Galaga, *what else is out there for the taking?*

I went back to work on my list, realizing I needed a bigger dream, a longer list. The first entry on the updated list was easy. Next to *No. 1*, I wrote: *Play Major League Baseball!* Playing college basketball came next, followed by representing the United States in soccer at the Olympics. Other goals were about personal development—attend and graduate from mainstream schools, get an A in English, and eventually go to college. Others were family based: getting married, having children.

I folded up the list and slid it under my mattress, a place where nobody would know about it but me. Whenever I accomplished a goal, I would take it out and make a check mark. Remembering how much my *Galaga* conquest meant to me, I included seemingly low-level accomplishments, like catching a ten-pound bass. But every goal was a step on the road to becoming the person I wanted to be. It was like my own hierarchy of needs.

Making goals became a habit that I incorporated into every baseball season. Each year in Spring Training, I would knock out a checklist of objectives, benchmarks I wanted to reach during the upcoming season. During my senior year of high school, my goal was to hit .400, and I batted .510. I don't believe that would have been possible without the power of goal setting.

For anyone who is reading this book—and especially for anyone working to overcome a disability or other obstacle in their life—I strongly encourage you to do the same thing. I continued to set goals throughout my big-league career, and I believe it was one of the prime reasons I was able not only to reach the major leagues but also to have such a long-lasting career.

CHAPTER 6

Family Plan

As a young child I loved visiting the small farm in Zanesville, Ohio, where my maternal grandparents, John Walter and Roma Curtis, raised my mom, Sallie, and her two brothers, Ronald and Monte. My mom told me that their move to "the country" gave her parents the opportunity to own land, grow their own crops, and have some livestock.

After the move, the local school became their biggest concern. As my mom told me, this was in the 1950s, and she and her two brothers weren't just the only African-American students in the school, they were also the only African-American family in their entire neighborhood. Even so, my grandparents were very happy after they moved to Zanesville. They enjoyed having their little farm and made good use of their land.

Some of my fondest memories came from fishing, boating, and just generally enjoying the atmosphere of a small town on visits to Zanesville. I believe that was the place I first developed my love of fishing and the outdoors. Zanesville was the first capital of Ohio, and today still has the world's only Y-shaped bridge that crosses two rivers, and we would frequently go to Putnam Hill Park to view the bridge. Sadly, like many Midwestern industrial towns, due to factory and store closings, people have been forced to leave Zanesville over the years. When my mom was growing up there, the population was about forty thousand. Now it is down to about twenty-five thousand.

My grandmother, Roma Curtis, was a real go-getter. After rising through the ranks of various jobs, she received her real estate license, and worked as a secretary at the Zanesville Campus of Ohio University.

My mom's father, John Walter "Buster" Curtis, was born and grew up in Marietta, Ohio. Marietta was founded in 1801 and is located on the Ohio River in Southeastern Ohio, on the border of Ohio and West Virginia. It is historically significant as the birthplace of the Underground Railroad.

My grandfather, whom my parents honored by giving me his last name as my first name, is still considered one of the best all-around athletes in the history of Marietta High School. His basketball skills were so exceptional that Parkersburg, West Virginia—whose high school was a longtime rival of Marietta High School—passed an ordinance prohibiting African-American players from competing against the all-white team of Parkersburg High School.

After high school my grandfather was signed to a contract by Olson's New York Harlemites, a semiprofessional all-Black traveling basketball team. The pay was one hundred dollars per week, which was great for my grandfather at the time. However, it was a challenging and exhausting experience. Most of the cities the team traveled to were segregated, which meant it was often difficult, if not impossible, to find an acceptable place to stay where the all-Black team could be served a meal. Also, the Harlemites did not have a team bus, and instead traveled from game to game via a caravan of several cars. My grandfather was one of the few players on the team who had a driver's license, so he was often driving many hours through the night after a game with little rest.

But there were challenges and indignities beyond the standard travel and lodging inconveniences for the Harlemites. When I was about ten, I remember my grandfather telling me a story about a game they played one night in a small town in Missouri against an all-white local team. The Harlemites jumped out to a commanding early lead, and the local crowd became extremely hostile and began shouting racial epithets and making threatening gestures. This was rural white America in the late 1930s.

The Harlemites coach called timeout, and the team decided the only way to guarantee they would get out of town safely was to allow the local team to win. So they proceeded to make unforced mistakes and miss shots intentionally, thus allowing the local team to come back and win. The local crowd was then very happy and gladly allowed the Harlemites to leave the town safely.

It was a deal with the devil, and throwing a game violated everything that is sacred about sports, but, as my grandfather explained to me, this was about much more than the outcome of a contest. This was about survival.

After a little over a year of this type of grind—and despite the money and his love for basketball—my grandfather decided to leave the team and return to Marietta. He then moved to Zanesville shortly thereafter, where he secured a job that he held for over thirty-five years at the Armco Steel Mill. It was there in Zanesville that he met his future wife, Roma Redman, to whom he was married for more than forty years. Together they raised three beautiful children, one of whom is my mother, Sallie.

As great an athlete as my grandfather was, and with his strong interest in sports, it saddens me that he didn't live to see me play professional baseball. In fact, he passed away while I was in middle school, so he never even got to see me play any of the three sports I excelled in at John F. Kennedy High School.

My family's athletic prowess came to me through my grandfather and my dad, who taught me how to play baseball, making sure I understood all the game's nuances. It was essential that I knew what I had to do, and where to be at all times. Because of my deafness, I could not rely on teammates or coaches to shout out an adjustment and instead had to be fully prepared in advance for any eventuality. I'm sure I was the only six-year-old who knew the infield fly rule before he ever set foot on a baseball diamond.

Because my dad taught me so many things about baseball, I

developed a habit of being well prepared that spilled over into all aspects of my life. Preparation went a long way toward my good fortune in sports, but I was blessed with natural athletic ability that, other than genetics, I couldn't quite explain. I was one of the better players from the very start and never quite knew why. When I played soccer, my teammates were excited because I was helping the team win by scoring a lot of goals, and my athletic ability helped me make friends.

I was always more of a participant than a spectator. Maybe because my deafness prevented me from hearing the captivating play-by-play of entertaining broadcasters who made watching games so appealing to others, I was never drawn to baseball on TV the way so many of my friends were. The Baltimore Orioles played a mere fifty miles away from the house I grew up in, but I didn't follow them very much because I was always busy playing outside.

My father took me to old Memorial Stadium in Baltimore for my first game when I was about nine years old, and I was thrilled to be in a big-league ballpark. We sat in the upper deck, a million miles from the action, but I really enjoyed seeing baseball played at the highest level and eating ice cream and hot dogs. It was a great day.

To this day I love being around people, in crowds and big cities. Some people have told me it's because deafness brings with it a certain loneliness, but I don't agree with that theory. Because deafness is all I know, it does not feel anything other than normal. I think the reason I love being among people is because I am not overwhelmed with the constant noise of the world. Since I am not inundated with the background sounds of a television, a radio, or even the conversation at the next table in a coffee shop, when I engage with people, it's a welcome respite from my own inner dialogue and any conversation we engage in is both purposeful and meaningful. People are never a burden to me.

As for engaging in spectator sports, I always watched the NBA more than any other sport, as I was a big Los Angeles Lakers fan growing up. I loved, too, watching the Dallas Cowboys football team on Sunday afternoons, back when their star players were Tony Dorsett, Roger Staubach, Everson Walls, and Drew Pearson. I had a Magic Johnson poster on my wall, along with a Lakers team picture, and a Dallas Cowboys Cheerleaders poster. The fact that I liked the Cowboys, not the hometown Washington Redskins, can be traced to the first time I watched them play on TV. The moment I saw that star on the helmet, I was hooked, and the Cowboys were my team and are still my favorite NFL team.

While my deafness has undoubtedly played a role in the fondness I have for being around people, it has also caused me to cherish time spent alone. I have found that reading is a great tool if you have a hearing disability because, in addition to being time well spent, it puts you on equal ground with the rest of the world. Still, I didn't read very much when I was a kid. My mom was always prodding me to read more because it was a great way to build up my vocabulary, but I was never really drawn to books until I was much older. Much of my syntax came from interactions with people, lip-reading, and watching movies, particularly after the advent of closed captioning when I was nine or ten.

CHAPTER 7

Kennedy High

Because of my hearing disability, I always felt like I was different for all the wrong reasons. At John F. Kennedy High School, I started to receive notoriety for my athletic achievements that extended far beyond the local playgrounds and, for the first time, began to feel different for all the *right* reasons.

I began to excel in athletics and people I didn't know would wish me good luck, congratulate me on a good game, or pat me on the back in the hallways. The positive reinforcement—acceptance for the first time—drove me to work harder, to be even better on the playing fields and in the gym.

I began attending Kennedy High School as a ninth grader in 1982. This was after one year at Colonel E. Brooke Lee Middle School, where I was part of one of the most dominating sports years in Montgomery County sports history.

The 1981–82 E. Brooke Lee teams went undefeated in soccer, basketball, and track and field. I was one of a group of talented athletes who composed those teams, and a team leader in all three sports, especially basketball and soccer.

The reputation for athletic prowess I established at E. Brooke Lee followed me to Kennedy High and, for the most part, I lived up to that reputation. I was a four-year starter in baseball and a three-year starter in basketball and soccer.

By the time I graduated, I had broken virtually every school record for all three sports, as well as the Montgomery County records for soccer goals scored in a single season (thirty) and high school career (sixty). I think both of those records still stand today.

As a senior I hit .509 for the baseball team, averaged more than twenty points per game for the basketball team, and scored thirty goals for the soccer team. Schoolmates weren't the only ones to take notice; local newspapers began to write stories about me, and scouts from the next level of all three sports began to reach out to me.

Considering my long career playing professional baseball, it's probably going to surprise a lot of people to learn that in high school, soccer was my best sport. It was the game I practiced more than any other, always kicking the ball around with my friend and neighbor Randy Hurowitz. Randy was the goalie, and I always pretended I was Pelé. He was my guy—he was so natural, so beautiful, and so graceful. I wanted to take the essence of Pelé and carry it with me everywhere I went, from the soccer pitch to the classroom and beyond.

Other than watching highlights of Pelé and having fun at the local park with Randy, I didn't follow soccer that closely and certainly didn't have any early formal training. Nevertheless, for reasons that are still not entirely clear to me, I was a natural at the sport. People frequently compared me to Pelé, which was the greatest compliment anyone could imagine. I wasn't the next Pelé, but I was a natural born scorer, and had a knack for always being in the right place at the right time.

My athleticism played a role in my success, of course, but I think my sense of direction, and innate understanding of time and space, factored too. So much of soccer is about seeing things before they happen, sensing how the game will unfold before it actually does. Being a visionary. Because of my deafness I am always aware of my environment, always using my peripheral vision to size up a situation, and always envisioning what might happen next. My deafness forced me to develop senses and skills I did not know I possessed, and the development of those skills turned out to be great preparation for soccer.

There is not that much verbal communication between players, which helps validate my theory that soccer is the sport where hearing is the least important. The game is spread out over a huge field, so vision, instincts, and conditioning are paramount, and hearing is virtually inconsequential.

In basketball, conversely, the game is played at such a fast pace and in closer confines, and that amplifies the importance of oral communication. Teammates calling for the ball, calling plays, and changing plays are a big part of the game. As the point guard I would constantly look to the sideline for my coaches, who would hold up fingers to indicate a changed play. On defense I could not hear teammates call for a screen or a change in defense, so I had to be doubly aware.

At Kennedy I began to look toward the future. I had to consider which sport could carry me the furthest personally and professionally, and I wondered if I should give up the other sports to give myself the best chance to reach the highest level of the sport I chose to focus on.

It was an easy decision: I wanted to play all three sports in high school.

By now, it was clear that the sport in which I had the greatest potential was soccer. Second was baseball. At the same time basketball was the sport I most wanted to play in college. But in 1982—and still today—U.S. professional soccer had a much lower financial structure compared to baseball and basketball. Plus, while I loved basketball, I was realistic about my prospects for an NBA career.

In baseball I had an arrangement with my teammates that, when playing in the outfield, if I called for the ball, it would automatically be my ball. There would be no confusion, no uncertainty over who would take it. Conversely, if a teammate knew he had the best play on a ball, he would wave his glove to call me off. I had to make sure and look. This simple arrangement makes me wonder why all players don't do a similar thing with their fellow outfielders because I never had a collision.

But soccer was a sport made for a deaf person.

Between my junior and senior years of high school, the United States U-16 National Team took notice, inviting me to try out for the team that would compete in the Under 16 World Championship tournament in Beijing, China. The first tryout camp was at East Stroudsburg University in Pennsylvania, and it was one of the first times I was away from home on my own. I was thrilled to be invited, but I never expected to make the team. Because I had such low expectations, I had a terrible tryout. It was also the first time I was exposed to a huge, regional tryout and I was overwhelmed.

I missed four easy scoring opportunities, the kind I always buried, because I was so nervous. I just wasn't myself, but the coaches were evaluating players on talent and potential, not merely on performance. Thankfully, I made the first cut.

My game wasn't nearly as refined as the other players, who probably had been given a lot of private coaching, and were technically advanced, while I relied on God-given ability. The staff could see I had some natural talent and must have believed they could make me a better player.

A few weeks later, we went to the United States Olympic Training Center in Colorado Springs, Colorado, for the next round of tryouts. Colorado Springs was the most beautiful place I had been to, at that point in my life. The training center was near the United States Air Force Academy, where the air is clear, and the mountains are gorgeous. Right away I felt at home in Colorado Springs.

I was more relaxed this time and played okay, but did not think I had shown enough to make the team. I went home happy for the experience, but ready to devote the rest of my summer to baseball, when I got a call telling me I had made the cut. There would be one more tryout, at the C.W. Post Campus of Long Island University, in Brookville, New York. The top forty players selected would then stay on Long Island for additional tryouts before the final team boarded a flight to Beijing for the tournament.

Being invited to the final tryout did wonders for my confidence and I arrived in New York with my spirit soaring. Then they had me play as a midfielder, instead of striker. I was terrified because I had never played midfield before. Striker was the only position I knew, scoring the only skill I had developed. I took my lumps, and it looked like I didn't belong. Then the coaches moved me up to forward, and I scored a couple of goals. I was just happy I was able to redeem myself and wouldn't have to leave Long Island licking my wounds. I was sure I wouldn't make the team. There were so many talented players; I just wanted to give it the best shot that I could.

When Coach Angus McAlpine read the names of the players who had made the team, my heart started pounding. I never knew what obstacle might appear in my never-ending battle to communicate, and Angus presented one I didn't see coming. Angus was from Scotland and had a strong brogue accent that made his lips move a little differently, and I couldn't always read his words.

Then the kid I had traveled to the tryouts with patted me on the shoulder and said, "You made the team." As soon as Angus finished announcing the names, I realized the guy I traveled with didn't make the team. I didn't know how to react; I was happy for myself and sad for him.

I had to ask him to call my family to give them the news. Asking a friend to make a call to my parents informing them of my good news was one of the hardest things I had to do, because I knew he would be calling his family with his own bad news. After the roster was finalized, we stayed at C.W. Post for an additional week of training, then flew to China.

When the tournament began, the faith Angus showed in me paid off. I was determined to make him look good for believing in me and was even more resolute in my desire to do the United States proud. I had played for neighborhood Little League teams, among friends in the schoolyards, and for my high school, but seeing *USA* on my jersey made me feel like I had the entire country on my side.

We played Guinea in the opener, and they were very fast and physical. We lost, 1–0. It was the most physical game I ever played in, with the Guinea team pulling my shirt, tackling me, and double-teaming me. At one point, when I was involved in what could have developed into an excellent scoring opportunity, a player tripped me on purpose and the referee didn't call it. I got so frustrated that I kicked a defender. Nobody saw it, but I still felt bad about it. It happened in the heat of the moment, but I didn't feel like I had gotten away with something. Instead, I was embarrassed and felt I had let the team down.

In our second game, we played Bolivia, a tournament favorite. They had Marco Etcheverry, who went on to play seven seasons as a star in Major League Soccer for D.C. United. We got behind early and trailed, 1–0. At halftime Angus ripped into us. In all my time playing different sports, I have never seen a coach so angry. We responded by coming out on fire in the second half and rallied to beat Bolivia, 2–1. I assisted on the game-tying goal, making a head pass to Larry McPhail, who put it in the back of the net. It was about a twenty-yard shot. That tied the game, and I later scored the game-winning goal on a give-and-go play.

Then we played the host team, and, with the crowd behind them, China beat us, 3–1. China scored three goals in the first ten minutes of the game, and we were all intimidated because the home crowd was so loud. How loud? So loud that it was the first time I ever played where I could sense the roar of the crowd and feel the stadium vibrating. I scored our only goal in that game, but it was not enough, and we didn't make it out of the round-robin portion of the bracket. For the tournament I scored two goals and had an assist.

Visiting Beijing was a wonderful experience, and it had a profound, unexpected effect on me. It was the first time I traveled out of the United States, and it was an eye-opening experience to be in a culture where everything was so different, from the language to the food. Seeing China stirred an emotion in me that I didn't realize existed. Before that trip I thought an afternoon tour to Washington, DC, was momentous. Otherwise, I was quite content to play sports with my friends in Silver Spring.

All that changed over the course of ten days. We went to the Great Wall of China, which remains the most amazing place I have ever seen. It was extremely steep, and thousands of miles long. Our trainer told us not to walk too far because you would get short of breath. The event kicked off with an opening ceremony near Tiananmen Square, where Li Xiannian, the president of China, welcomed the teams from all over the world.

When I got back to Maryland, I added a new entry to my list of goals: see the world. Reentry into normal life was also a bit challenging after such a high and I experienced a bit of a hangover. That listlessness was only temporary. Shortly after the tournament I was named by *Kick!* magazine as one of the top fifteen youth soccer players in the world, which was a big boost to my confidence—not just in soccer, but also in all the sports I was playing.

I didn't know if soccer could be in my professional future, but for the first time, I believed I could compete on a global stage, and that if I trained hard and played smart, and with passion, people would take notice. First it was Angus McAlpine, and then it was the people at *Kick!* magazine.

I became a new person on the pitch, too, playing a different brand of soccer. I had learned a few skills, and became a more polished, more technical player, instead of relying solely on my instincts and natural athleticism. My coach at Kennedy, Jeff Schultz, was impressed and told me I had become a completely different player. I was more accurate in my passing and shooting, and more selective, shooting less than the previous season, but I still scored more goals because I picked my spots.

I was now recognized as a world-class soccer player, but in the United States in the 1980s, that offered no guarantees. It was becoming apparent that baseball was the sport that might have the most to offer me professionally. By my senior year big-league scouts descended on Kennedy High School. The Pittsburgh Pirates, St. Louis Cardinals, San Francisco Giants, Baltimore Orioles, and New York Mets all sent scouts to watch me play.

This was a big deal. I had gotten noticed in Beijing, but that was soccer, which didn't carry the same impact in the United States as baseball, which has long been referred to as "our national pastime." Young baseball players can be drafted in the Major League Baseball Draft a few different times: after their senior year of high school, after attending a junior college, or after their junior year of college. During my senior year high school baseball season, it became obvious that I might be drafted.

A scout from the San Francisco Giants was the first to come and see me. Since the Giants were the first team, I was afraid they would be the last if I didn't look good. So I was nervous, as if my entire future was at stake. They ran me through a private tryout, where they had me throw, tested my speed at sixty yards, and had me hit. Despite my anxiety I did well, and felt good about it.

The Pittsburgh Pirates also showed interest and invited me to a regional tryout camp in Northern Virginia, one of several they held across the country. I performed well there, so they invited me to participate in a national tryout at Three Rivers Stadium in Pittsburgh. It was intimidating to be on the field with all the other talented high school ballplayers, but I was the fastest guy there. I also threw well, and hit okay, so my confidence soared. What I remember most was the awesome feeling of being at Three Rivers Stadium. I didn't want it to be the last time I had that feeling.

Through it all, the New York Mets were the team that expressed the most interest in me and, more importantly, my post-baseball future. A Mets scout named Bob Dawson had come to several of my high school games. As a result of his assessments, Bob's supervisor with the Mets, Carmen Fusco, arranged a private, individual workout for me.

The private tryout took place on a field in Frederick, Maryland.

I had a soccer game earlier that day and suffered a lower back and leg injury, but I was determined to show up. I limped through the entire workout, but Carmen was impressed that I tried out, despite being hurt, and later told me that he saw uncommon, innate athletic ability in me. He invited me to Shea Stadium in Flushing, Queens, New York for a private tryout.

My dad and I went to New York, and along with Carmen there were several other high-level Mets executives at the workout. As I recall, Frank Cashen, the team's general manager was there, along with Roland Johnson, the director of scouting, and Steve Schryver, the director of minor-league operations. I was very nervous and intimidated because I was the only player on the Shea Stadium field, but my lower back and leg injury had fully healed by that time, and the workout went extremely well.

The whole day was like being at a Mets fantasy camp. I walked into the dugout and picked out Howard Johnson's bat from the rack. Mets legend Bud Harrelson threw me batting practice. I crushed one homer all the way into the upper deck in deep right field. They tested my speed, and I could sense that also impressed them. They had me throw from right field. They also wanted me to take some ground balls at shortstop—a position I had never played before—but I still looked like I knew what I was doing. When it was over, I felt like I had already played for the Mets, like I might play for them again.

As the draft got closer, it began to look like it would come down to the Mets and Pittsburgh. The Pirates told me they were prepared to draft me in a relatively high round, but only if I would commit to forgoing college and immediately begin my professional baseball career. That was a deal breaker for me.

While Major League Baseball scouts were assessing how I would fit into their organization's plans, I was trying to determine which organization fit best with my plans. I had already been through the recruiting process for college, and now professional baseball teams were talking about drafting me. With my parents' guidance I decided that I would complete all four years of college and not leave early to play a professional sport.

During my high school career, I received over one hundred letters from colleges expressing interest in me for baseball, basketball, and soccer. But basketball remained my top priority for a sport to play in college. I wanted to attend a school relatively close to my home, and one that also has a strong reputation for academic excellence. That narrowed my list of potential choices significantly.

At the time the National Collegiate Athletic Association (NCAA) allowed prospective recruits and their parents to accept up to five paid visits to college campuses. But my parents and I decided that we would not accept a paid visit invitation from any college that I wasn't seriously interested in attending. We recognized that these paid visits can be fun, but why allow a university to spend money on our family when there was virtually no chance I would be attending that college?

A fortuitous combination of events led to my college selection. Between my freshman and sophomore years at Kennedy High School, I attended a summer basketball camp at Our Lady of Good Counsel High School, a private Catholic school then located in Wheaton, Maryland, and now located in Olney, Maryland. The basketball coach at Good Counsel High School, Bernie McGregor, was also the operator of the camp. Coach McGregor and I bonded immediately, and his camp was an extremely positive experience for me. The bond was so strong that I came very close to accepting an invitation from Bernie to transfer from Kennedy to Good Counsel. It was a tempting invitation. Good Counsel is a member of the Washington Catholic Athletic Conference, which is arguably one of the best in the entire nation for high school basketball. But as tempting as Coach McGregor's offer was, I decided to remain at Kennedy.

However, the relationship between my family and Coach McGregor continued while I finished high school at Kennedy.

When Coach McGregor accepted a position as assistant basketball coach at the College of William & Mary (W&M)—and indicated that he and head basketball coach Barry Parkhill wanted to offer me a basketball scholarship—it was practically a done deal.

Attending a college with a strong academic reputation was a priority, and W&M had that, and then some. In fact, in 1985, Richard Moll, the dean of admissions at the University of California–Santa Cruz, wrote *The Public Ivies: A Guide to America's Best State Colleges and Universities*. In this book Moll created the term "Public Ivy," and identified eight schools that provided similar prestige and academic rigor as the actual eight Ivy League schools. The College of William & Mary is prominently included on that list as a "Public Ivy."

Our visit to the campus of William & Mary in Williamsburg, Virginia, is the only paid recruiting trip that my parents and I accepted. We had earlier taken an unpaid trip to the University of Virginia, but I got the sense that their interest in me for basketball was minimal. It is ironic, however, that when their assistant basketball coach, Jeff Jones, was taking us around the campus, we were spotted by Bruce Arena, who was then Virginia's head soccer coach, and later became the head coach of the U.S. national soccer team. Bruce immediately recognized me, and said he was surprised and happy to see me on campus. I then subsequently received a scholarship offer for soccer from Virginia, with a guaranteed walk-on for the basketball team. As tempting as it was to see if I could successfully compete in basketball in the Atlantic Coast Conference, I remained firm in my commitment to William & Mary.

When we took our official visit to W&M, my parents and I were impressed with everything. Most notable was our meeting with Dr. Carroll Hardy. Dean Hardy, as she was most commonly and affectionately known, was the dean of students for multicultural affairs and special needs. Our meeting with Dean Hardy left us firmly convinced that I would receive all the necessary support to accommodate my deafness.

With Dean Hardy's commitment, and Bernie McGregor there as almost a surrogate father, there was only one other consideration before I officially enrolled and started classes at William & Mary. My parents and I informed Coach Barry Parkhill that we anticipated I would be drafted in baseball and requested permission from him that, should that happen, I could try to work out a deal that allowed me to play baseball professionally, while at the same time remaining eligible to play college basketball. When Coach Parkhill agreed to the terms, a major domino had fallen into place.

Now came the hard part: convincing a Major League Baseball team that allowing one of their prized prospects to prioritize college made for a good investment. In trying to negotiate this seemingly impossible deal with organizations that had become accustomed to grooming incoming talent like new recruits, who were assigned to basic training, then methodically worked their way through the ranks, my father had one ace up his sleeve. He was a true believer, convinced beyond any doubt, that a well-educated, well-rounded, and mentally sharp prospect would pay great dividends, both on the field and in the clubhouse, even if it meant that player's development deviated from standard operating procedure.

As draft day got closer, things were heating up. Like a scene right out of *Jerry Maguire*, my father stepped in, telling both the Mets and Pirates that I had accepted a basketball scholarship to William & Mary. He warned them that I wouldn't forgo college to go pro, no matter where I got drafted and how much money I was offered. That scared off the Pirates, who wanted me to focus on baseball full-time.

That left the Mets. My father wasn't bluffing. Again he told them not to waste their time drafting me if they wouldn't allow me to go to college in the offseason. After many long conversations, the Mets reached an agreement with my dad that they would not only draft me, but also allow me to become a part-time minor-league baseball player in the summers, while at the same time continuing to be a full-time student-athlete at the College of William & Mary.

At that time NCAA rules allowed an athlete to compete as an amateur in one sport, and also play professionally in a different sport. But the NCAA rules did not allow a college athlete to be under contract with a professional sports team, while at the same time be on scholarship at an NCAA member institution.

Thus, to fit within the confines of these rules, we agreed that each of my four years at William & Mary, I would miss the first part of the minor-league baseball season and only report to my team in the Mets organization after the school year ended. Prior to the start of the academic year at William & Mary the Mets would give me my unconditional release so I could go back on my basketball scholarship there. And then I would sign again with the Mets before I reported to my assigned team for the next baseball season. Obviously, for this arrangement to work, it required a total commitment of faith and trust from all the parties, and I will be forever appreciative to the Mets and Carmen Fusco and Roland Johnson for what they did.

Years later, Carmen flattered me when he said, "It was risky, because it was sign/release, sign/release, sign/release, sign/release, but I knew Curtis had the integrity to honor the deal." The feeling was mutual. With Carmen representing the Mets, I had complete faith that they would also honor their half of the deal.

Getting to the big leagues never comes down to one day, but June 2, 1986, was pivotal. It was three days after my high school graduation when the phone rang. My dad picked up, and it was the Mets letting us know they had drafted me in the tenth round.

We were celebrating my sister Jacqui's birthday when I learned the news, so I didn't want to celebrate too much and take the shine off my sister's celebration, but I couldn't help myself. A high school player insisting on going to college normally scares off teams from drafting him, so I was thrilled beyond belief to be drafted in the tenth round. So was Jacqui, and everyone in my family.

My mom started calling people to share the good news. She wasn't really informing them as much as thanking them because everyone I knew had a hand in my success. Ken Rippetoe was the baseball coach at Kennedy, and he really helped me. Ken seemed to see something in me before anyone else, constantly encouraging me and going the extra mile. He would throw me batting practice until the sun disappeared. Then he would get up early the next morning and do it all over again. Steve Grupe, my best friend, also played a big part in my success. Without him, I might not have achieved the academic success that I did. He was one of the first people I called to give him the news.

High school was an important time for me because it was my first taste of success that reached beyond the small scope of my neighborhood and the Wheaton Boys Club. I made the *Parade* magazine All-American team for soccer, and I was the Army National Player of the Year for soccer.

I was never cocky, always humble; I think that was one of the things people liked about me. That came from my parents, who were both great role models. They pushed me to be the best person I could be and never treated me any differently than my sisters. They were very supportive of everything I did. They criticized me if I needed it, and ultimately they shaped me into behaving the right way on and off the field.

Before high school I knew nothing of the far-reaching expectations that my growing profile in the community would bring. Friends, neighbors, and even strangers expected a lot from me. When the widespread attention of being a high school star came my way, I knew how to handle it because I had been around it all my life. My father had an impressive job, pulled down a nice paycheck, and had a way of making friends in a hurry—people just liked being around him.

Yet, despite all my father's accomplishments, he never acted like a big shot, he was just my dad. He is one of the smartest people I have ever known, the kind of person who always has an answer for everything. When we watched *Jeopardy!* together, it was almost as if he had been given the answers in advance. He taught me how to handle success, even when I had none. He saw something in me that I didn't.

Even after playing hundreds of games in the major leagues, the compliment I enjoyed most from the managers I played for—several of whom are all-time greats—is that Curtis Pride played the game the right way.

CHAPTER 8

Minor Leagues, Major University

Two weeks after my high school graduation, my parents drove me to Kingsport, Tennessee, where I was to begin my career as a professional baseball player. They dropped me off at a low-budget motel, where the Mets' youngest minor-league players were housed, both thrilled and terrified that their deaf son was about to be on his own, making his way through the world of minor-league baseball. I know they felt that way because I was wrestling with the exact same emotions, and I could see all my hopes and fears reflected on their faces.

I'll never forget standing on the balcony of the run-down motel room that was now my home, waving goodbye as my parents got in their car and pointed it back home to Maryland. It was as if they had dropped me off on another planet, and now they were taking the spacecraft back to Earth, leaving me stranded in this strange, new world.

Rookie Ball was about learning to be an adult, about being away from home and on your own, as much as it was about developing your skills as a professional baseball player. My teammates and I all stayed at that same motel, and there were frequently groupies hanging out in the lobby, around the pool, and at the bar. The groupies all wanted to hook up with the players and I just couldn't wrap my head around that. Several of my teammates were doing drugs, smoking pot, getting drunk. Then they would take the groupies back to their rooms. I had always been firm in my commitment that drugs and alcohol were not for me, and now I was coming to the realization that tawdry sex was not my cup of tea, either.

This was another one of those times when I believe my hearing disability worked in my favor. Because I had to work extra hard for an opportunity, I wanted to devote all my attention to baseball and not let the opportunity slip through my fingers. For many of my teammates, things had always come so easily that they became complacent, believing they could devote half their time to baseball and the other half to fun—and still be successful.

I was paired in a room with James Morrisette, a teammate from Alabama, who had turned down a football scholarship at Auburn in favor of baseball. James was a pretty good player and probably could have worked his way to the big leagues, had he been more focused. However, he got caught up in the lifestyle and never made it to The Show. A couple of years later, James and I got to be good friends in high-A ball at Port St. Lucie, Florida. That's where I came to realize how fortunate I was to have my father cut the deal with the Mets that allowed me to pursue my college education in the offseason.

Later, one of my teammates at Kingsport was Lee May Jr., the son of Orioles and Reds Hall of Famer Lee May. He was the Mets' first-round pick in my draft class (twenty-first overall), but only played in the minors for three more years after Kingsport and then was released without ever playing even one game in the big leagues.

Less than five percent of Major League Baseball players have four-year college degrees, and there were others in the game who envied me because I was able to negotiate a deal where I was allowed to go to college full-time and also play minor-league baseball. Had I not gone to college and instead focused solely on baseball, my career might have been different. I might have gotten to the big leagues sooner, might have stayed longer. I will never know for sure, of course, and I don't care. What I do know is that had I not made it at all, I would have hit a dead end. If my two children are ever in a similar situation, forced to choose between college and professional athletics, I will strongly advise them to prioritize college.

In minor-league baseball so many of the players just want to have fun when they should be working. It was easy to get caught up in a situation where they could not resist the drinking, the drugs, and the groupies. They chose the instant gratification of fun over working to get better for the long term, and they had no idea how much they would regret it later.

The Rookie Ball season is short, designed just to give players an introductory taste of professional baseball after the draft. My Rookie Ball season was winding down, and I had learned a lot about life, but my game suffered, and the end couldn't have come soon enough. In forty-six at bats, I hit a pathetic .109, with one home run and four RBIs. Now I was going back to school, where I would devote myself to the numbers that mattered most to my parents: grade point average, or GPA.

Baseball had helped forge my identity and self-worth and now it was threatening to destroy it. Because I had overcome the low expectations of others and excelled on the baseball diamond, I had reason to believe I could do the same thing in the classroom. It really made me think I could fit in anywhere. That's how powerful baseball had been to my self-image. But now, since I hadn't done well in my first season of professional ball, I also began to have doubts about my ability to compete at the next level in academics. Baseball had been at the heart of everything I accomplished, and now I was petrified my struggles would have a carryover effect, turning the game I loved into a source of additional failures.

Swapping bats for books had become a rite of fall, but this time it felt very different. I no longer had the security of my parents' suburban house or the freedom that life in the minor leagues offered. Worst of all, my normally unshakable confidence was showing cracks.

Most of the big-league baseball scouts had wanted me to go

directly from high school to professional baseball, forgoing college altogether, and I was beginning to understand why. They knew the physical demands of the game and the academic requirements of college life did not coexist easily. They also believed that if you wanted to get to the big leagues, baseball had to be the first thing, the last thing, and the only thing in your life.

Thankfully, my father was able to negotiate the unique arrangement where I would play minor-league baseball only from May until August. If I earned good grades in college, I could continue in professional baseball, but my parents told me if I was unable to stay on track toward earning a degree in four years, they would step in and insist I give up baseball. When I agreed to that deal, I was riding high, and my confidence was unshakable. Now that I was facing adversity, part of me was starting to regret the arrangement.

Arriving for my freshman year at William & Mary was like being called up to the big leagues of academia. Two days removed from cohabitating with beer-drinking, skirt-chasing jocks in a run-down motel with wall-to-wall beer-stained carpeting in Kingsport, Tennessee, I checked into a dorm of perfectly groomed, preppy, scholastic overachievers at what had been named one of America's top educational institutions a year earlier.

I was eighteen, unsure of my place in the world, having been unsuccessful in my first season in professional baseball, a failure that, if it continued, could change my education from nicety to necessity. Baseball had been my one true superpower, and if I couldn't make it in the low minors of the sport I believed I was born to play, how could I possibly make it at the upper echelon of academia? The more important earning a degree became, the more uncertain I grew of my ability to compete in the classroom.

I drew inspiration from my surroundings. The W&M campus was so gorgeous and historic that I wanted desperately to make it a place where I belonged. For an eighteen-year-old college freshman, I had already experienced a lot of diverse life experiences. I'd played in charming and historic ballparks, traveled to China to play soccer, and had been recruited at impressive places. But nothing made me feel like I was joining an exclusive club quite the way William & Mary did.

People have a perception of deafness as something that affects your intellect. It does not, of course, but old stereotypes die hard. My parents knew a degree from one of the best schools in the nation would be a quick and effective defense against anyone who doubted my intelligence. My mom and dad always insisted I go to college, and if not for their guidance, I would have signed with one of the professional baseball organizations that wanted me to focus solely on baseball, forsaking college altogether. My parents did not give me that option, and not a day goes by that I don't appreciate their foresight. They knew education was important and my deafness only served to up the ante.

The course of their lives had been changed by higher education. After growing up in blue-collar Youngstown, Ohio, where his parents did not finish high school, my dad became the first member of his family to graduate from college. My mom graduated from nursing school and went on to a long career as a nurse. School had been good for them, and they wanted their kids to have the same advantages.

My two sisters both excelled in college—Jacqui at the University of Maryland, and Christine at the University of Missouri, where she majored in journalism at one of the best programs in the nation. Christine worked for many years as a book editor at several of the top New York publishing companies and is now a highly successful independent book editor. She is also an accomplished author herself, with her first book, *We Are Not Like Them,* with coauthor Jo Piazza, having been released to wide critical acclaim in 2021. Christine and Jo followed it up with a second well-received book, *You Were Always Mine,* released in 2023.

While my parents were the driving force in my pursuit of a formal education, I had plenty of my own incentive, too. My deafness had always given people pause: Is this guy a little slow? Does he lack focus? Can he keep up? In time I could win most people over, but a William & Mary degree would accelerate things, providing indisputable validation of my intellect. A little slow? *It just so happens, I'm a graduate of an Ivy League–caliber college,* I could say. I never wanted to throw academic achievement in anyone's face, but I liked the idea of having incontrovertible proof of my intelligence in my back pocket, just in case.

My first day on campus, I checked into my dorm and met Greg Taylor, my roommate. Greg would be a teammate on the basketball team, until back injuries forced him into a medical retirement from playing basketball. I had always imagined my roommate would be a friend, confidant, and family member all rolled into one, but Greg and I did not have that kind of relationship. The rooms were so small, you could practically reach your arms out and touch both walls, making it difficult for two people to coexist without irritating one another. Our schedules and priorities never quite clicked: If I was studying, he was looking for fun; if I wanted to stay up late, he wanted lights out. We never meshed and eventually we decided to go our separate ways.

The dorms at William & Mary were an altogether different atmosphere than staying with minor-league teammates in motels. While the minor-league players were living like there was no tomorrow, the students in the dorms were looking at the big picture, working hard to set themselves up for the future.

Fortunately, I was always as much a student as I was an athlete—my parents' influence rubbing off on me. They say you are whom you surround yourself with, and luckily for me, it was the studious, plan-for-your-future mentality of the school year that got inside me, while the live-for-today baseball mentality never took hold.

The typical William & Mary student had scored 1400 or more on their SATs and been academic stars of their high school class. They seemed to be gifted with intelligence, then worked hard to go the extra mile, a combination that got them to the top of their class.

It was the same formula I worked to my advantage on the athletic field; I was a natural athlete, but it was all the extra work I put in that enabled me to reach an elite level, so I felt a commonality with the student body.

Now my challenge had been turned upside down. I had to rely almost solely on hard work to compete in the classroom. My motivation, however, did not waver. I always liked the story of the tortoise and the hare because I felt like I could relate to the tortoise. I was never the smartest guy in the room, but I had a dedication that resulted in slow and steady progress.

I had a two-hour study table with the basketball team every day. After that, I would go back to my dorm room and study some more. Time management was paramount, as sometimes I couldn't follow along if the professor looked away or turned his back to write on the blackboard. After class I had to read the transcribed notes, so it took me twice as long just to absorb the material, and that meant I couldn't waste a lot of time.

It's funny, but because of having so little time, I became much more efficient at time management than I ever would have been. Once again my inability to hear turned out to be a hidden asset, teaching me to become more efficient in all aspects of my life. Academics were just another example.

After I finished my homework, I could spend time with my friends in the dorm. But until I finished my schoolwork, I would not socialize. That was the deal I made with myself. Once I was done studying for the night, I'd play cards, watch TV, talk with my hall mates, and hang out.

Smart, funny, and passionate about learning, Dr. Carroll Hardy made me feel like I had an angel looking out for me, making sure I went to class, got good grades, and had a true collegiate experience. Dean Hardy was a strong African-American woman, and I know she must have faced obstacles of her own as she ascended in academia. The road she traveled could not have been an easy one, but she had the courage to be a strong role model. She constantly assured me I could make it in college, that I could do whatever I wanted, become anything I desired. She did everything she could to make sure I got the best education possible and made sure I graduated. I will forever be in her debt for everything she did for me. Dean Hardy passed away in 2012, but anytime I think of William & Mary, I still see her, in her office, encouraging a student to aim high and make the most of their time on campus. Without her support, I know I would not be as successful as I have become.

Dean Hardy wasn't shy about demanding I meet with her once a week, in her elaborate office. "I want you to get your ass in my office every week," she would say. "I'll walk you to class if I have to." You didn't mess with her.

I would tape my lectures and have somebody transcribe them. Back at Kennedy High School, I had an interpreter, so this was a new system for me. I never fell behind, never had any trouble. I always made sure my professor knew about my situation beforehand. If I had an issue, I would ask my classmates to go over the material with me.

At the same time Dean Hardy was helping me find my footing on the academic side, basketball practice began. Unfortunately, I got the feeling the basketball coach, Barry Parkhill, was more interested in his players staying eligible than he was in seeing them get a strong education.

I've always loved biology, with science being my favorite subject in high school. My first year, two fellow freshmen teammates were allowed to take biology, but Coach Parkhill wouldn't let me take the same course, and that upset me. He thought it would be too hard for me. It was insulting. If you were letting my freshman teammates take biology, why couldn't I take it, too? It seemed like he didn't trust me, and that hurt.

Since my teammates were allowed to enroll in the class, I felt this was clearly about my deafness. I was told to take psychology, instead, and I wasn't happy about it, so my response was to fail that class on purpose. I only showed up half the time and didn't put any effort into it outside of the lectures. I'm hardheaded and I wanted to send a message to my coach that I cared about academics just as much as, if not more than, athletics, and that I am not deaf and dumb. I believed I should have been able to take whatever courses I wanted to take, just like anyone else.

I failed the course on purpose to make a point, which hurt my chance to make the honor roll. Being stubborn was not the right course of action, but my message was received. Coach Parkhill responded by allowing me to take any course of my choosing, but I did not feel good about what I had done. Neither did the people around me.

The assistant athletic director was upset with me because I had failed the psych class on purpose, and he was afraid I would not be eligible for the upcoming basketball season. Every time I saw him, he kept asking me if I was passing all my classes. It was demeaning, but I had brought it upon myself.

More importantly, my parents were also very upset with me, and that is what hurt the most. They did not know what I had done until they saw my fall semester transcript with two A's, one B, and an F. They had thought my GPA would be higher, and when I told them what had happened, they laid into me. It takes a lot to make my parents mad, but I had found a way to do it. It was the only F I ever got in school, and they could not figure out why I did that to myself. In sports it would be called an unforced error, the kind top athletes are taught to avoid.

I was so discouraged by the incident that after my freshman season I considered transferring to Georgia Tech. But, before I made my decision, Coach Parkhill was fired, and replaced by Chuck Swenson. Chuck had been a team manager for Bobby Knight's 1976 national champions at Indiana and went on to be an assistant for Mike Krzyzewski at Duke, but had never played college basketball. Despite his lack of playing experience, I really liked the fact that he had learned under Coach K at Duke, and that was enough for me to stay at William & Mary.

Chuck Swenson was not a bad coach, but we had different philosophies. The first couple of years playing for him went well enough, but by my senior year, things took a turn for the worse. We did not have a great relationship, which led to him benching me. It was very frustrating. I'm stubborn and he was, too. I think he knew it would help the team if he played me, but he refused to do so. I had made the conference all-defensive team and the all-freshman team, but because he did not recruit me, he didn't feel like I was his guy. He had no investment in me.

I was a professional baseball player, and that distinction forged a unique identity for me on campus, but I had to remember that basketball was paying the freight. Without my basketball scholarship, a struggling minor-league ballplayer would never have been able to afford an elite private education, so basketball could not be a part-time job. It had to be my everything, even if it really wasn't. In truth, academics were my top priority, and staying in shape for baseball was second. Basketball was probably third on my hierarchy, but I did love the game, so much so that I continued to play when I probably should not have.

During my freshman season of basketball, I was stunned when I started having heart palpitations. My heart rate would spike to nearly two hundred beats per minute, something that caused me to hyperventilate. I couldn't control it and I would get sick during games, often vomiting. One time I passed out. I was terrified. I was afraid there was a chance I could die. I can be blasé about my hearing disability and the challenges it creates, but I pay very close attention to all other aspects of my health.

Our team doctor was very reassuring and sent me to a cardiologist in Richmond, who ran all sorts of tests. My heart was stimulated, to see how it would respond, and they performed an electrode catheterization. Despite all the tests they could not replicate the symptoms.

Ultimately I was diagnosed with tachycardia arrhythmia, a condition the doctors said I was born with. They told me it was not life-threatening, but even so, I had to sign a waiver absolving

William & Mary of any liability if anything serious happened to me while playing basketball. My parents weren't too happy about it, and I decided to stop playing soccer. With all the cardio associated with the sport, it was a risk I did not need to take.

My heartbeat would fluctuate every time I played hard, and the cardiologist gave me three options: I could have surgery to correct the problem, take medication every day for the rest of my life to control it, or leave it alone.

Because it was not life-threatening, I opted to leave it alone and, over time, I learned to control it. I became adept at managing my breathing and pacing myself on the court; I knew when to go hard, when to ease up. If I felt tachycardia arrhythmia coming on, I would raise my hand and the coach would take me out. It was never a problem in baseball, just basketball; and at eighteen I felt self-management was an easy choice. No way was I opting for elective heart surgery, and I didn't want the side effects of medication, so I learned to cope with it. The Mets knew about it, but it was never a problem in baseball. It was physical activity that triggered it, not nervousness. Once I knew how to manage it, it was no longer a problem.

I will always look back with fond memories of my time in college. After four years at William & Mary, I left with a degree in finance, a lot of great friends, and, most importantly, the restored confidence that I could make it anywhere.

CHAPTER 9

Binghamton Blues

I had a college degree, but I still couldn't graduate from the minor leagues of professional baseball. I had climbed through the Mets' farm system slowly, but not steadily. Three years at Kingsport; one each at Pittsfield, Massachusetts; Columbia, South Carolina; and Port St. Lucie, Florida. I hit a respectable .284 in 1988, but that was in my third year of Rookie Ball, which did not exactly make me a phenom. Now, in my seventh year of professional baseball, I was twenty-three years old and stuck at Double-A level Binghamton, New York, unable to make much headway on my big-league dreams. In my heart of hearts, I began to wonder if it might be time to drop out of baseball.

But I kept all that to myself. I had made a habit of calling my parents at all hours of the night, typically after one of my games, and a call usually meant that things had gone well.

If I had performed poorly, I was more apt to turn inward and brood. I didn't want to burden anyone with my insecurities, and I was desperate to create the impression that I was doing well, and everything was under control, even when it wasn't. So I waited until I had something positive to report before phoning home. Back then, there was no satellite TV coverage of my minor-league games, and no Internet for my parents to track my progress, so news arrived directly from me or not at all.

My father anticipated good news when he picked up the receiver on a humid July night, but he could tell immediately that this call was different, even through the TTY machine. He knew I had been having a difficult season, but I don't think he was prepared for my level of despondency. I certainly wasn't. I'd been depressed about my career before, but things had never gotten so desperate that walking away seemed like the only way out.

My typing on the TTY that night was shorter and crisper; finally I stopped mincing words and got to the point. I typed into the machine: *I'm quitting.* I was two years removed from earning a degree in finance from William & Mary, and until that season I seemed to be on the way up. Now I was stalled, and in the back of my mind, I envisioned my education rescuing me from the uncertainty of it all.

For the past few seasons, the good times far outweighed the bad and my numbers had gotten progressively better. Little by little, I allowed myself to believe I might actually have a shot at making it to the major leagues. I'd followed up a disastrous .109 batting average, in my first professional season at Kingsport, by hitting .240 in my second year there, and then upped that to .284 in my third professional season, so I was trending upward. After that season I was named a top ten prospect in the Appalachian League.

When I moved from Rookie Ball to Single-A, my average slipped to .259, but that wasn't unusual for a player moving up a class, so the Mets didn't seem overly concerned. A year later, that faith paid off and I was able to lift my average to .267 at Single-A Columbia.

A year prior to arriving in Binghamton, in fact, I had made the All-Star team while playing at St. Lucie of the Florida State League, hitting .260 with nine home runs and thirty-seven RBIs in 116 games. Historically, the Florida State League has always been considered strong for pitchers, so my statistics compared very favorably with other top prospects in the league. I was feeling good about my career, having fun, and forging a reputation as someone who played the game with uncommon passion.

At Binghamton I was only making about $1,200 a month, and after paying my rent and taking care of meals and expenses, there was very little left over. Still, I didn't care. Finances had never been a driving force in my life, and I felt extremely lucky to be playing professional baseball. Most of my friends from William & Mary were now pulling down good salaries in the business sector, but many of them told me they would have gladly traded places in an instant.

When the season began, I wouldn't have traded my baseball career for any amount of money. I was getting the opportunity to pursue my dream, and the monetary cost of chasing that dream was irrelevant to me. I spent less time looking at the numbers in my checking account than the ones on the stat sheet, which was a good thing because in 1992 I owned the clothes on my back, an Isuzu Rodeo SUV, and nothing else.

Minor-league baseball is about development and learning how to adjust, almost as much as it is about results, and the Mets liked the fact that my numbers showed I was improving as a hitter and had an aptitude for adapting to different situations. How well a player had performed wasn't nearly as important as how well he was projected to perform, and I was still viewed as a prospect with potential.

It's counterintuitive, but for a baseball prospect, Double-A is in many ways more crucial than Triple-A. It's where a lot of careers stall and I knew my first season with Binghamton would be a pivotal year in my career. I was determined to make the most of it. I started out hot, hitting over .300 the first couple of months.

Things could not have been going any better. It looked as if my stay at Binghamton would be a simple matter of climbing another rung on the ladder. Then everything started falling apart. My struggles began off the field. I had been dating a girl from my high school. We started out as friends, and shortly after graduation our friendship developed into a romance. But the prolonged separations we endured during the baseball season eventually took a toll on the relationship. While I was off playing baseball, my girlfriend broke up with me unexpectedly in a phone call, and my game went in the tank.

I didn't want anyone to know how fragile I was, so I didn't open up to anyone. But I was torn up inside. Trying to break into the major leagues felt like trying to crash a party without an invitation, but I always felt I could win people over with my exuberance if they got to know me. Being dumped hit hard because my girlfriend knew me better than anyone, and now she was no longer in my corner. It was irrational, but I began to believe if a girl back home could bail on me, there was no reason the Mets wouldn't do the same thing.

So I started pressing, trying too hard to make an impression. When I was at the plate, I still believed my deafness wasn't necessarily a bad thing because without the sounds of the game, a passing airplane, or the crowd noise to intrude upon my concentration, I was able to focus entirely on the pitcher without so much as a hint of distraction.

Remember the movie *For Love of the Game?* In that movie Kevin Costner played an aging pitcher who, in his last appearance, was pitching a perfect game for the Detroit Tigers against the New York Yankees. When he came out to the mound for the ninth inning to try to complete his perfect game, for dramatic effect, the producers of the movie eliminated all the sound of crowd noise to emphasize how Kevin's character of Billy Chapel was focused only on the one important thing of throwing his best possible pitches directly to the catcher. I love that movie because, many times, that is how I felt, being able to focus entirely on the pitcher without any distraction from outside noise. But now, for the first time ever, I carried a suitcase full of distractions with me to the batter's box.

Baseball can be as easy or as difficult as you make it, and I had always been able to simplify things. But at Binghamton the game was becoming complex. In the best of times, my technique at the plate was simple. I had trained myself to pick up the ball about two or three feet after it left the pitcher's hand. After the ball was released, I would watch it pass through an imaginary circle, and then, almost instantaneously, I would determine on what plane the ball was traveling. That was the key: If the ball stayed on a level plane, it was probably a fastball, and I'd stay back and attack it. If the ball changed planes, chances are it was a curveball or some other off-speed pitch, and that meant continuing to track the ball's path before I determined if it was hittable. Because I have 20/20 vision and no distractions, picking up the ball and tracking it always came easy to me.

Only now I was making things hard.

I had repeated my technique so many times, that once I got to the plate and locked in on the pitcher, the process was intrinsic and muscle memory took over. But even my most basic instincts were failing me now. I was still free from the distractions of the ballpark, but I was carrying other baggage to the plate with me, and it began to weigh me down. Anxious to climb out of my prolonged slump, I fell in deeper and deeper, and it felt like I was thrashing in quicksand.

All the clarity that had enabled me to block out the world was now clouded. As I battled the worst batting slump of my career, it was compounded by a case of homesickness, which was brought on by the end of my first real romantic relationship. I began to wonder how much patience the Mets would have with me.

My playing time started to diminish, and it was becoming apparent that the Mets' belief in me was fast eroding, too. My own self-confidence would be the next thing to evaporate. Because so many people had doubted me and refused to take my aspirations seriously when I was growing up, I had always been afraid that if I didn't take my career seriously, no one else would, either. I also wondered, deep down, if I really belonged in professional baseball. This introspection led me to become my own worst critic. I had always set high goals and often placed unrealistic demands on myself, and now I was approaching every at bat as if my entire career hung in the balance. I was overthinking and overanalyzing everything.

My mental struggles were combined with the fact that I wasn't getting consistent playing time. I couldn't find a groove on the field, and I couldn't find a comfort zone in the clubhouse. The Binghamton Mets were on their way to the Eastern League Championship, and in a curious way the team's success only served to aggravate my struggles.

We had a great team, but I didn't feel like I was part of it because I didn't play in every game. I felt even worse because the team was doing well, and I wasn't helping. I know how much fun it is to win a championship and I didn't want to bring anyone down, so I tried to be as supportive as I could be, but that's all I had to offer.

When you are a deaf player making contributions, you not only feel like one of the guys, you also feel special. But when you are not contributing, you feel like a charity case. I felt like the batboys and clubhouse attendants might even be more important to the team than I was.

When I turned to my teammates for support, I didn't always find it. During that summer the clubhouse at Double-A Binghamton wasn't necessarily the best place to look for help. In the best of circumstances, a baseball clubhouse can be a clubby, collegial fraternity of brothers. But, like kids thrown together for a season on MTV's *The Real World,* or different personalities living together on CBS's *Big Brother,* a minor-league clubhouse can also turn into a place of insecurity and deceit.

As my average dipped, my frustration soared. I was battling a batting slump and personal problems, and now I was battling myself, too. Throughout T-ball, high school, and college, I had always tried to be open to whatever suggestions my coaches made, but I had become distant and difficult to reach. Due to my frustration I was being obstinate. When people tried to help me, I wouldn't let them. I began to think my career was coming to an end. I felt guilty that part of me, maybe, wanted it to end. That seemed like the easiest way to stop the pain and frustration.

Our manager was Steve Swisher. He would arrive at the park early, and, under the sweltering midafternoon sun of upstate New York, take me to the batting cage for one-on-one tutelage, trying to fix my erratic swing. I loved playing for Steve. He wanted me to get better as much as I did, which makes him a perfect player's manager.

Steve believed that players who worked hard deserved to be rewarded, and he didn't mind putting in extra hours to try to help me break out of my funk. As we worked together, we developed a close relationship, and Steve became one of my biggest advocates in the Mets organization. I was grateful for all he did for me, but felt bad that I couldn't repay him by breaking out of my slump.

Steve told me some things that still stay with me. I remember him saying, "Curtis, if you start quitting now, you're going to quit everything else in your life. It'll become easy." It was simple advice, but it resonated deeply and kept me going.

Steve was a first-round draft pick in the 1973 MLB Draft and had a successful nine-year big-league career, including being selected to the 1976 National League All-Star team, so he certainly had a lot of credibility in the world of professional baseball, and I very much valued his advice.

Still, it was as if my downward spiral was stronger than my manager's desire to pull me out of it, and no matter how much time and help Steve gave me, it didn't change things. I had always been determined, and now I was being determinedly stubborn. Deep down I wondered if part of my subconscious wanted to fail, if being sent home by the Mets would be the best thing that could happen to me because it would prevent me from being labeled a quitter. But on a conscious level, I wanted to turn things around, even if I felt like I was pounding my head against a brick wall.

Steve kept trying everything he could to help me. But the extra hours I spent in the batting cage under his direction didn't help, because my problem wasn't at home plate as much as it was on the home front, and in the home clubhouse. Steve knew I had broken up with my girlfriend, and he tried to tell me that when something like that happens, it happens for a reason, and that I should move on. I appreciated what he was telling me, but it didn't change how I felt.

I finally reached my boiling point in the clubhouse after another hot summer's night spent working too hard to find something that had always come so easily. As I sat on a stool in front of my locker after another night with too many strikeouts and too few hits, a pair of teammates believed my struggles were cause for jocularity, and that my hearing disability would shield them from any response from me.

When teammates didn't like me, they saw me as a piñata. They felt they could wind up and take their shots with no fear of reprisal; and to some degree I was responsible for that perception. I was so determined to be a good teammate and a good organizational guy that I didn't want to make waves. So I made a habit of turning the other cheek, even when I should have pushed back.

I could always tell if people were making fun of my deafness, even if I didn't hear them. Sometimes people made fun of me face-to-face, and when they did, I could read their lips. Other times they mocked me, and I could read their body language. There were times when word would get back to me through friends or teammates. But I always knew.

Finally, after a game in Binghamton, the abuse coming from inside my own clubhouse went even further than ever before. While I was sitting on a stool in front of my locker, a pair of teammates began making fun of me. One held his hand over his ear, taunting me for my hearing disability. They thought they were so clever when they did that. Did they have any idea how many times I'd seen it before? Another teammate began making fun of my speech impediment by imitating the speech pattern I had worked so hard to make as clear and audible as I could.

I felt like I was right back on the playgrounds of my childhood. As a member of the New York Mets organization, I couldn't bring myself to believe that professional baseball players in their twenties were dishing out the same treatment I'd received from elementary school kids. I never expected my own teammates to make fun of me. I thought at that level everyone would be old enough to be beyond that kind of childish behavior. For the most part my teammates always had been more mature, whether they were Little Leaguers or players who were in a league of their own.

Dealing with the abuse had a way of thickening my skin. Much the same way I had learned to be disciplined and selective at the plate, I had also become pretty good at laying off the slings and arrows of the assorted hecklers that always seemed to turn up. I had learned to treat insolence the same way I dealt with a fastball too far inside: I'd just dust myself off, step back in, and go about my business as if nothing had happened.

My parents had trained me to lay off the verbal brushback pitches. While my father had enlightened me on the value of self-defense, he believed a physical response to a verbal assault should be the exception. In all other instances my parents preached a dispassionate, reasoned, and articulate response.

"People that make fun of you aren't worth your time," they told me whenever I would come home upset and in tears, which was often. I tried to take to heart my mom's advice to "just ignore them."

But parents don't always heed their own advice and mine were no exception. One of my first experiences with taunting in professional baseball came when I was playing for the Columbia Mets in Fayetteville, North Carolina. My parents had driven down from Washington, DC, excited to see their son play against high-level competition. They took seats along the third-base side, not far from where I was stationed in left field, and soon after, the ball was hit to me. I misplayed the ball, and a fan behind my parents started making fun of me, yelling, "Hey, Helen Keller, are you deaf and dumb, or just dumb?"

I knew people often would call me Helen Keller, the renowned author and activist who gained notoriety as the first deaf and blind person to earn a Bachelor of Arts degree, but it was the first time my dad got wind of it. He did not take it well. It was meant to be an insult, but to me, being compared to Helen Keller, and all she accomplished, was a compliment. But this moron was mean-spirited, and he meant it as an insult.

The guy wouldn't let it rest, but after the second utterance of "Helen Keller," my dad had heard enough. He stood up and got in the guy's face. "That's my son," my father said. But after my dad sat back down, the fan started mocking me again, closing his eyes and flailing his arms like he was lost in the dark. Another fan saw it, got a police officer, who then stood under the bleachers, watching the jackass carry on.

My dad saw the cop and baited the guy. "You got anything more to say about my son?" The guy stood up, went back into his Helen Keller act, said something else to try to get on my dad's nerves, and the cop intervened, ultimately escorting the guy away and out of the stadium.

At one point my mom had to hold my dad back to stop him from fighting the guy. But even if my parents were not able to always follow their own advice, they did a good job of drilling the message into me as if they were throwing me batting practice.

I learned to respond to taunting with the same detached, methodical approach I took to hitting. I could see the insults coming, like a baseball on its way after being released from a pitcher's hand, and I had learned to lay off the pitches in the dirt. But this incident in the Binghamton clubhouse was different than the others. Not only had baseball always provided a refuge, but I had always gone out of my way to treat teammates like family members. Now that sanctity was being shattered, so I felt compelled to respond. I was pissed off.

When I was back on the playgrounds, I lacked the confidence and oral skills to respond to harassment verbally, but I now had both the diction and the backbone to walk up to those two knuckleheads and address them face-to-face. Like a manager bolting from the dugout to dispute a botched call, I exploded from the stool in front of my locker, stormed across the crowded clubhouse, stopping only when I was within spitting distance of my tormentors.

"I don't appreciate what you're doing," I said, my voice now rising to match my level of anger. "We're supposed to be teammates, but you're both selfish and immature."

Though I felt unburdened by the outburst, I had the feeling that the spoken warning would merely be the undercard. Clubhouse arguments were not uncommon, and I was prepared to add to my message by backing it up with a smackdown. My hands were balled up in fists, my chest heaving as I took deep breaths. Adrenaline was flowing through my body. It was the same exact way I felt before I beat the crap out of that schoolmate back home for the same kind of teasing.

But the more I spoke, the more I reflected on how much I had developed, as both a speaker and a person, and how much time and energy I had expended to educate myself and fit in with the auditory world. I had established my oral skills and vocabulary so I could express myself, and it dawned on me that I could deliver a much more powerful message with a silver tongue than I could with golden gloves.

I also knew that if I reacted to ridicule at age twenty-three, the same way I had at the age of eight, the intervening fifteen years would have been a waste of time. So instead of taking a shot, I delivered a parting stab: "I can't hear you, but I can feel you. My handicap is deafness. Yours is stupidity and intolerance. I'd rather have mine."

Then I just turned and walked away. As I did, I remembered a simple lesson my parents had taught me: When people make fun of you, don't lower yourself to their level. It would be the easy thing to do. But have enough respect for people not to do that. If I had caused the situation to escalate, I would have been worse than they were.

There were a couple of teammates who were nice enough to let me know that the guys making fun of me didn't matter. Dave Harris, our first baseman, was supportive, and Tim Howard, who played third base and the outfield for us, got angry at them, and I appreciated that. After admonishing my teammates for their juvenile behavior, I went home, plugged in my TTY, and dialed my parents' house, sending out what was essentially a call for help.

Between Steve Swisher and most of my teammates, I knew I had people in my corner. Yet, my inability to respond to their help left me feeling a little guilty, as if I were letting them down. Finally, in reaching out to my parents, I turned to the people who had always provided me with the answers.

After hanging up the phone, my parents loaded up their minivan and hit the road for upstate New York. They'd made similar trips countless times, usually bringing friends and family members, and turning my games into a weekend-long party, but this one must have felt more like a rescue mission than a summer holiday. Mom and Dad left home Saturday morning and drove straight to my game that night. When it was over, they took me back to their motel room and listened as I told them about my problems.

That night I received one of the most pivotal pieces of parental advice I ever got, in an inconsequential motor inn located near a minor-league ballpark, at a time when absolutely nothing made sense and no one else could get through to me. My father didn't get angry with me, and I appreciated that. He stayed calm and I think that made me more receptive to what he was saying. I think my father knew that parental approval had always been an essential part of my motivation.

As I sat on a bed in my parents' cramped motel room in upstate New York, my father offered a simple message: "You can quit if you want to, but you can't quit in the middle of the year like this. You've earned a college degree and there's a lot you can do with your life, so if you want to give up baseball, that's your decision. It's just not a decision you can make right now because you've signed a contract for this season, and you need to honor that contract. I didn't raise my son to be a quitter."

That brief conversation was all it took to remind me of how much baseball meant to me. It also reminded me of how much my name meant to me. It made me realize that whenever I saw it on a jersey, on a locker, or on a glove, I wasn't just playing for myself, I was playing for Pride. My entire family was there with me, and that made the load lighter.

A day later, my parents got back in their van, waved goodbye, and left Binghamton, thinking that maybe they had seen me play professional baseball for the last time. I stuck around and played out the season, but finished the year with a miserable .227 batting average, while striking out 110 times in 388 at bats. It was a thoroughly forgettable season, and when it finally ended, I was convinced my career had ended right along with it.

After we won the championship, everyone went out to celebrate at one of those small taverns that minor-league ballplayers love. It was about the size of a double-wide trailer, jam-packed, and I could tell by the way it vibrated, it was very loud. I wasn't crazy about the place, but I loved being with my teammates, loved talking baseball. Everyone was drinking and having fun, but I was worried about my future and unable to enjoy the moment. I was about to become a free agent and I wanted to know if I figured in the Mets' plans. It would have been more fun to celebrate with the other players, but I didn't feel like I had contributed anything and was concerned that I was running out of time with the Mets organization, so I cornered Jim Duquette, the Mets' assistant minor-league director, and put him on the spot.

"Do I have a future with the Mets?" I asked. I know Jim was surprised by my directness. We were supposed to be celebrating, not talking business.

Jim said he wanted me back, but he couldn't guarantee playing time. He didn't know what the Mets' plans were, but if I wanted, I could come back. He was insinuating that I was on my way out, trying to let me down gently. But I couldn't take the hint, so I came right out and asked him: "Do I have a better shot signing with another organization?"

"Yes," he finally said, and now it was clear I needed to look elsewhere.

The next morning I loaded up my car and made the five-and-a-half-hour drive back to my parents' home in Maryland. Three months shy of my twenty-fourth birthday, I moved back into my boyhood bedroom, unsure of my future, but convinced I'd struck out at baseball, and that my dream of making it to the major leagues would never come true.

CHAPTER 10

Playing with Purpose

Feeling defeated and deflated after my disastrous season at Binghamton, I arrived back home humbled, and took an offseason job as a teacher's aide at Kennedy High School, my alma mater. However, this didn't feel like an offseason job as much as a career change and I liked it. I helped kids with disabilities do their schoolwork, helping to make sure they were getting the most out of the class.

The kids didn't know I played professional baseball until the teacher told them. They didn't believe it at first, but then they started asking me questions about my baseball career. I had come off a bad year in Binghamton, been through a bad breakup with my girlfriend, and had teammates making fun of me. It was easily my worst season ever and I wanted to walk away. Working at Kennedy High School seemed like a good place to hide. As much as I enjoyed the work, deep down I knew I was going backward because I didn't have the strength to move forward.

The kids were kind of awed by the fact that I played professional baseball and started to gravitate toward me. My status as a baseball player created a level of trust and they opened up to me, let me into their circle, and I was able to reach them. Things changed for me when they realized I was on their level. That's when I knew I wasn't alone. Even though I had a bad year in Binghamton, they were looking up to me because I was doing something that I wanted to do. At least I was trying. That had a profound effect on me. If I quit, what kind of role model would I be?

I decided to again devote 100 percent of my passion toward baseball and worked out hard that offseason. In baseball every year is a long journey, with its requisite ups and downs, but you find a way to get through it. I got through it with the help of those kids. Also, my high school baseball coach, Ken Rippetoe, spent countless hours working out with me in the offseason, for which I will always be grateful.

You must be mentally strong, that's the key. "Be mentally strong" is a mantra I constantly repeat to myself. It starts with a strong belief in yourself. My experience with the kids at Kennedy helped me remember an experience I had during my first year in pro ball in Kingsport, Tennessee, and I began to connect the dots, realizing there was great power in connecting with people.

I had received a letter from a girl named Amanda. It was one of my earliest pieces of fan mail, and I stared at it in disbelief, unable to comprehend the idea that someone I had never met knew my name and felt compelled to write to me. Finally I pulled up a stool in front of my locker and opened the letter. Amanda wrote that she was legally blind, and I was her favorite player. The letter was so amazing that I believe it's important to include it in this book. Here, with her permission to reprint it, is the entire letter Amanda wrote to me:

> *Dear Curtis:*
>
> *I am writing this letter to tell you how much I like to watch you play baseball. I am a 12-year-old girl, but please read my letter anyhow!*
>
> *My mom takes me to your home games, and she told me you wear a hearing aid on your left ear, so I guess you are handicapped like I am.*
>
> *I am legally blind, but I can see a little bit. I sit in the corner of the stands and when you are getting ready to*

bat, I can see your numbers on your shirt. I can't see home plate but my mom tells me what happens so I will know when to cheer for you.

I always wanted to play ball, but I was scared because I don't see good. But I watched you play, and you did good, so I decided to try.

Mom found a t-ball team and they let me play. I can see the ball on the tee, and I bat left-handed like you. A coach on first base calls to me when I hit the ball and I run to his voice until I get close enough to see the base. Then they tell me when the next batter hits and I run to the second-base coach's voice until I can see the base. And that is how I play. So, I wanted to thank you for helping me try.

I will come to all your home games if I can. I am going to middle school next year. School is hard.

I have a special machine to help me read and write.

I wish you lots of luck. I will watch your games and you will always be my favorite player.

Your friend,
Amanda

Amanda lived near the ballpark and her letter was so moving that I invited her to attend as many games as she wanted. Amanda's relative was Dusty Rhodes, the famous New York Giants outfielder, and she had the game in her blood. She loved being at the games and became a regular, sitting in the first row behind the backstop.

I was thrilled that I had inspired Amanda, that her circumstance had a clear parallel to mine. I never had a player with a disability to pattern my own game after, so I decided to embrace the idea of being Amanda's role model, to treat every game as if someone was looking to me for guidance. I thought it was important to show that people with disabilities can do whatever they want *if* they believe in themselves, work hard, and don't worry about what other people think. I wanted to make an impact on as many people as possible. Amanda showed me that while my job was being a baseball player, I could be much more than that.

Later, after I had successfully turned my career around, the media picked up on my status as a deaf person in professional baseball, and the fan mail started to pour in. I received hundreds of letters, many of them from people with disabilities or from parents of kids with physical or mental challenges. I tried to respond to all of them, thanking them for their support and telling them how grateful I was that they considered me an inspiration. More than anything, I wanted them to know that they held the key to their own success—and once they began looking at the world as a place of possibility, not of impossibility, everything would open up for them.

That first letter from Amanda, and the bonds I established with the students at Kennedy High School, contributed significantly to my decision to give my career one more chance. More importantly, it made me realize that I could be a success even if I did not reach all my goals. My friendship with Amanda further opened my eyes. I decided I owed it to people who were looking for a nontraditional role model to share my story, and to do so, I had to talk about it.

Just like many other people, public speaking was never my thing. I remember when I was a freshman at Kennedy High School, I had to give a speech in my English class and I was terrified. I was extremely shy, afraid the other kids would not understand my diction. I didn't have confidence in myself and that was my biggest obstacle.

The topic I chose for my speech was how to use jumper cables to start a car. I rehearsed intently, as if prepping for opening night on Broadway. I had that thing down pat. I wore my favorite gray T-shirt to class that day, just to make sure I was as comfortable as possible. As I was giving the speech, I got so nervous that I began sweating profusely. You could see the color of my T-shirt go from a light gray to a hue so dark it could have passed for black. As soon as the bell rang, I raced home to shower and change my clothes.

Over time and through repetition, I learned to control my emotions and nervousness so that I would be able to speak to larger groups of people. Today I still get butterflies before a public engagement, but that's part of the thrill of reaching out for a connection. Addressing a large group of people is much easier because I'm used to it. Like hitting a curveball, it all comes down to practice and conditioning.

I have had the privilege of being a featured speaker everywhere from high school banquets to corporate seminars to big-league clubhouses, and it's always an honor, but it's also a responsibility that I take seriously, so I take time to practice what I plan on saying. Being well prepared is the best remedy for fear.

From that first season at Kingsport, all the way through my big-league career, I was regularly approached to do interviews or speak with a group about being a deaf baseball player. It was never a burden, and I didn't mind missing a little extra pregame practice because I knew I had a chance to make an impact.

I was very fortunate in that the media always treated me well, probably because they liked my story, and it gave them a break from writing only about the games. My success on the baseball field was an easy, feel-good story, and the writers and broadcasters always felt good about telling it. They felt like they were bringing something important to the public. Although I was often asked the same questions, repeatedly, I never got tired of answering them because I knew it might be my only chance to reach people. Since making it to the big leagues seemed like such a long shot, I believed minor-league baseball might be my only chance to offer a ray of hope to other people like me.

In the world of people with hearing disabilities, my encouragement meant as much to the parents as to the kids, because they were worried about their children's future. Then they met me.

"Wow," they'd say, "you went to college, got a degree, and you are playing professional baseball. All things are possible."

A lot of the deaf kids I met used sign language, so I had an interpreter help me, but we also communicated through body language. I could tell what they were thinking or feeling by their body language. It became obvious to me that I could have a special connection with them because, unlike any other player, they could quickly sense that I understood exactly what they were going through because we shared the same disability.

So many parents of deaf kids told me they couldn't find anyone their kids could look to for optimism, and I desperately wanted to assume that role. At the time I was still only playing in the minor leagues, but I was getting along fine in the hearing world and believed I could be an example of fitting in with the hearing world.

Working that offseason at Kennedy High School helped me remember how far I had come. Working with those kids reminded me that if I quit, I wouldn't just be quitting on myself, I'd be quitting on everyone who ever believed in me.

CHAPTER 11

Baseball Bliss

Rejuvenated and inspired, I left Silver Spring for Spring Training in Florida to start anew. After shopping my services during the offseason, only the St. Louis Cardinals and Montreal Expos made offers. I had signed a free agent contract with the Expos and now I was off for their camp in West Palm Beach, Florida. It meant beginning again with an organization that had no prior investment in me, but I didn't care. I was primed and ready to take another shot, energized by those kids back at Kennedy High School.

I went to the Expos' minor-league Spring Training camp, and they assigned me to the Double-A Harrisburg Senators of the Eastern League. I was disheartened that I wasn't invited to the big-league camp, but not entirely surprised. The Expos, like every team, were more interested in the development of players they had drafted, partly out of loyalty and partly due to confirmation bias. They wanted to prove they were right to draft them in the first place. There were times when I thought proving a deaf player could not make it in the major leagues was part of a confirmation bias, too. But I had a lot of speed, and I began earning respect when I was clocked at 6.2 seconds in the sixty-yard dash, swifter than Rondell White, who was considered the fastest player in the organization.

All I knew about Harrisburg was that I had learned in third grade it was the capital of Pennsylvania. Yet, somehow, Harrisburg turned out to be the right place at the right time for me. In fact,

Pennsylvania's capital city soon became one of my favorite places to play, at least in part because of the ballpark's location along the Susquehanna River. For night games I would show up for work at 1:00 p.m., grab my fishing pole, and go fishing. The park was on an island, surrounded by water, and walking distance to great fishing spots made me feel like I had drawn up the plans for the place myself. Where else can you keep a fishing rod next to a bat in your locker?

We had a great group of guys on the team and the right chemistry was there, which was always the X factor for me. Fitting in and being accepted were the reasons I was drawn to baseball in the first place, and if I was treated as an outcast inside my own clubhouse, the game lost much of its appeal. Harrisburg reminded me of why I loved baseball, which was something I needed after my experience in Binghamton. Occasionally a teammate or two would grab a fishing pole and join me on the river, which was great for team morale, but even when I fished by myself, I enjoyed the solitude. I shared an apartment with Archie Corbin, who had been a teammate in the Mets system. He was from Beaumont, Texas, and he and I got along well.

I loved mostly everything about Harrisburg, especially the winning. In fact, as it turned out, we ended up having one of the greatest teams in minor-league history. The Senators finished fifty games over .500 (94-44) and won the Eastern League Championship, largely, I believe, because we were a team that liked each other and played together.

We had future major-league All-Stars Cliff Floyd and Rondell White on that team, as well as other future major leaguers, such as Shane Andrews, Joey Eischen, and Kirk Rueter. But even with all the great camaraderie and fishing, more than anything, I will remember Harrisburg as the place I first met our manager, Jim Tracy, who made a huge impact on my career and in my life.

Jim was incredibly patient and committed to making me a better person and player. Jim was a baseball man, through and through, but he was a people person, too. Those two characteristics didn't always coexist easily, with so many baseball lifers immersed so deeply in every nuance of the game, they could forget the humanity behind it. Baseball clubhouses could also be cliquish and fraternal, like you were pledging some secret society, but Jim was different. He knew baseball and he knew people. I liked him right away.

Jim had spent parts of two seasons with the Chicago Cubs, hitting .249 with three home runs in eighty-seven games before his big-league dreams came to an end at the age of twenty-five. I respected that he had reached the pinnacle of his chosen sport. But I also got the sense that Jim felt like he had left Major League Baseball with unfinished business, like he would be back in The Show someday as a manager. My instincts turned out to be correct, as Jim would work his way back to the top of his field, spending eleven years as the respected manager of the Los Angeles Dodgers, Pittsburgh Pirates, and Colorado Rockies.

More than anyone I had encountered, Jim understood me. He seemed to know how badly I wanted to make it to the Major Leagues and seemed to realize that it wasn't just for me, that others stood to benefit from my success, too. Years later, Jim would say there was something about me that he found challenging, something that made him want to do everything he could to help me succeed, to lift me to the next step on the ladder.

"Number one, Curtis made you appreciate what you had, but you also realized that this person you were dealing with was a very special situation," Jim would say, looking back on managing me. "This was a young man that was very committed to succeeding when a lot of people were saying, 'We don't think he can.' I was challenged by that. I knew this kid was committed to proving them wrong. I knew he had skills that would play on a major-league team."

Jim had such a good-natured demeanor, and he knew so much about baseball, that I found myself constantly sitting next to him in the dugout, quizzing him on game situations and strategy. I would ask him about baserunning, outfield angles, bunting, and he always had an answer. Without my realizing it, Jim was giving me a primer on how to manage.

No one was more dedicated to the game, but Jim also knew there was more to life than baseball. Once, on an off day, Jim invited me to join him and his wife, Deb, and their three sons fishing on a houseboat in Northern Ontario. Playing for Jim in Harrisburg, fishing before games and on my off days—it was everything I ever dreamed baseball could be.

Jim would later say that because of my speed, dropping down a bunt was the equivalent of a free pass to first base.

"I remember working a lot with Curtis in the early part of the day, and we spent an awful lot of time with him on his bunting. He was so fast, and he worked so hard at this and got it down. Anytime he made it a footrace between him and a pitcher, or involved a first baseman and a pitcher on a fielding play, he was safe every time."

With supportive teammates and an industrious manager, I felt comfortable. Those were things they say don't show up in the box score, but they did reveal themselves in my stats. I hit .356 with fifteen homers and thirty-nine RBIs in fifty games, quickly outgrowing the Eastern League. Much of that success could be attributed to my comfort level.

Jim also appreciated the fact that my deafness sharpened other skills. "Curtis had an unbelievable sense of awareness on the bases," he would say. "A great understanding of how, and when, to go from first to third. The visual perception that he had, because as a base runner, he couldn't hear the ball come off his teammate's bat. And knowing when to go from first to third, reading the body language of the outfielders, and the angles that the outfielders were taking and realizing the fact that he could make it easily to third. All those kinds of things."

One afternoon, a few hours before a game, the phone was ringing in Jim's office. I couldn't hear it, of course, but the minor-league director for the Expos, Kent Qualls, was beckoning. When Jim called me into his office, I had an idea it might be good news, but I almost didn't want it to be true. I'm not sure I fully comprehended the fact that I was about to be one step closer to my dream, one phone call away from the big leagues.

"You're going to Ottawa," Jim said, but it still did not register. It was a small step, going from Double-A to Triple-A, but an important one. Then he hugged me, and it all made sense. I was back on my way, climbing the ladder.

"That was one of the most gratifying hugs that I was able to give," Jim would recall. "I've given a few of them, but that one was really, really special."

I didn't want to leave. Walking out the door of Jim's office meant starting all over again, and right now, in the Harrisburg Senators clubhouse, I felt like I had found my place in the world—baseball, fishing, and terrific teammates. A wonderful manager. I thought about all the things I would be leaving behind and I was overcome with emotion.

I thanked Jim for all that he had done, for making me a better player, for creating an environment that brought a team together and fostered winning. Then I looked in his eyes. I could see Jim was fighting back tears, and so was I. They weren't tears of sadness because he would be losing one of his leading hitters. They weren't even tears of joy, either. No, these were different. His were tears of pride, the kind a parent cries when his or her child does something well. I could tell by the look on Jim's face that he saw me as one of his guys, like I was one of his sons. That's when I knew I had to go before I totally broke down myself.

I was reminded of the movie *An Officer and a Gentleman,* where there was a very emotional scene near the end. In the film Zack Mayo, played by Richard Gere, thanks his drill instructor, Sergeant Foley, played by Louis Gossett Jr., for helping him make it through officer candidate school. I thought about that scene as I parted company with Jim, trying futilely to find the right words to thank him.

I don't remember exactly what I said to Jim, but Zack Mayo's dialogue would have done nicely: "I won't ever forget you, sir."

As I look back, Jim Tracy was, without a doubt, one of the most influential people in my life.

CHAPTER 12

Feeling the Cheers

I hit the ground running in Triple-A, hitting .302 with six home runs and twenty-nine stolen bases in sixty-nine games, resulting in the unforgettable moment when Ottawa Lynx manager Mike Quade told me I was going to The Show.

The walk from Quade's office inside the clubhouse back to the team bus remains vivid, as if it happened in a dream. On the bus back to Ottawa that night, I couldn't help but think back on everything that led up to that moment. A vision of my early days on a Little League field, memories of my stint teaching at Kennedy High, and all those challenging times in the minor leagues flashed before my eyes, then dissipated as we pulled into the parking lot of Lynx Stadium at 5:00 a.m. I was stirred back to the present, as we were met by loved ones and the rising sun on one of those lazy, dreamlike mornings that you don't want to end. We all began to realize how close we had grown as teammates, how much we would miss one another, and how much we would all miss this chapter of our lives. Because it was time to say goodbye, doing so was the one thing nobody wanted to do.

But I was due in a big-league uniform in Montreal in eight hours, so as dawn broke over Canada's capital city, I hurriedly parted company with those who were now my former teammates. I knew I'd cross paths with a few down the road, but I also knew that because I had been called to the majors, their odds of making it had just gotten longer and that made the moment bittersweet.

Then I drove directly to the house I shared with my host family to pack my belongings. Everyone was still asleep, so I tiptoed into the house and gently walked down the creaky wooden staircase and into my bedroom in the basement. The clock was ticking, and I didn't want to be late on the first day at a new job, so there was no time to sleep. I had a lot to do, but I had to call my parents first. They were the people most responsible for my making it to the major leagues and I wanted to share the moment with them. I had always dreamed of paying them back for all their dedication to me by being successful, and this was that moment.

"Guess what?" I remember asking my father on the TTY machine, before answering my own question. "I just got called up to the majors." Again . . . called *up*. And once again, it was fitting because my spirit was soaring, and I was floating on air like one of those oversized balloons in the Macy's Thanksgiving Day Parade.

My dad was speechless. I remembered how he had taken the time to explain the rules of the game to his eager but naive six-year-old son. Now it was my turn to explain to him how big-league baseball worked.

"I got The Call last night," I said. "They want me to be in uniform today."

"The best phone call I ever got," my dad told me later.

That made us even. It was the best phone call I ever made.

The scouting reports on me had always emphasized my speed, and when I hung up the phone, I did my best to make those scouts look smart. Working quickly, I tossed two baseball gloves, two pairs of spikes, and two bats into a tattered, dirt-caked duffel bag, then crammed my wardrobe, which consisted solely of jeans, shorts, and T-shirts, into a lone suitcase.

Dressed in faded denim jeans, a gray T-shirt, and a worn-out pair of Reeboks, I threw the two bags, which contained all my worldly belongings, into the back of my SUV. While I was piling up hits and RBIs, my SUV was rolling up miles, taking me from my hometown of Silver Spring, Maryland, to minor-league outposts in Kingsport, Pittsfield, Columbia, Port St. Lucie, Binghamton, Harrisburg, and, finally, Ottawa. This time I fastened my seat belt, waved goodbye to my erstwhile hosts, got on Highway 417, and pointed my SUV in the direction of the major leagues.

The radio dial remained untouched and in the off position. That's one of the first things people notice when they ride in a car with me. It's normal to me, but other people always find it odd to have this brief sensation of deafness. I've always found that I do my best thinking alone behind the wheel of my SUV, traveling from town to town and team to team. With nothing but two lanes of blacktop and my own thoughts to occupy me for the next two hours, I stared at the Trans-Canada Highway in front of me, then peeked in the rearview mirror and watched as Ottawa was reduced to a fond memory and a line of statistics on the back of my baseball card.

I had never been to Montreal before, but I had been on the road to the big leagues for eight of my twenty-four years, and there was no way I was going to get lost now. Not that there was much chance of that happening. For some reason, I have been endowed with an uncanny sense of direction. I'm not sure why, but I could always find my way around a new city. When I was a small child, my mother often found herself asking me for help when she got turned around while taking me to one of my many practices, or if I was with her while running errands.

"It's just something you always had," my mother told me.

Alone on the road to Montreal, my mind began to wander again, just like it had on the bus the night before. I began to think about the people who had helped me take my baseball career further than it probably had any right to go. The closer I got to Montreal, the more I wondered if I had dreamed too big and if I was setting myself up for a fall. Although I tried not to display them outwardly, I was racked with self-doubts, and questions raced through my mind. Would I be able to hit big-league pitching? Would I fit in with the guys in a major-league clubhouse? I tried to tell myself the same thing I had told the kids back at Kennedy High.

"To be successful," I told them, "you must believe in yourself. Regardless of what you must overcome, you can achieve your dreams if you believe in yourself."

I reminded myself that I had to practice what I preached. I was playing for the kids back in Maryland as much as for myself, that I wasn't completely alone.

There are a lot of people who have been incredibly supportive of me, I kept telling myself in the seclusion and silence of the open road. *They want me to do well, so I'm going to do well for them.*

As Ontario became Quebec, and Highway 417 seamlessly merged into Autoroute 40, I wondered if my own transition would be as smooth. I didn't know what the Expos would expect of me, how much I would get to play, or what I could do to make a good first impression. I didn't want the drive to end. As long as I was envisioning life in the big leagues, I could make it perfect. Once I got there and it became real, would it live up to my imagination?

I did my best to put my apprehension aside and continued on, driving straight through. I was too excited to stop for gas or food, and as I rolled into the outskirts of Montreal, I thought not about how far I had come, but how much further I wanted to go.

It had been more than twenty-four hours since I'd slept, but I felt alert and wired as I pulled up to a guarded entrance in front of Olympic Stadium. "I'm Curtis Pride, the Expos' new player," I announced simply, trying my best not to sound like I was bragging, even though I probably was. After being directed to the players' parking lot in the ballpark's bowels, I negotiated an underground maze, then made my way to the Expos clubhouse.

It's customary for a new player to check in with the manager upon arrival, so my first stop was Montreal skipper Felipe Alou's office. Alou had a reputation as a soft-spoken player's manager, and much the same way that I could sense things on the playing field,

I immediately picked up a good vibe from my new manager. Felipe reminded me that baseball is a small world by sharing the memory of a time our paths had previously crossed, back in the low minor leagues.

"Florida State League, 1991," Alou said. "I was managing West Palm Beach; you were playing for the St. Lucie Mets; you hit one of the longest home runs I've ever seen."

I remembered, too, let out a sigh, and a relieved smile crossed my face. While playing in Single-A, I had squared a ball up, driving a tape measure home run over the batter's eye in center field, at least 475 feet away. It was the farthest I had ever hit a ball. Some say that at that time it was the longest home run ever hit in the history of the Florida State League.

"The next day," Alou told me, "I went out for a run and found the baseball in a field behind the stadium. I couldn't believe how far it went. Congratulations, and welcome to the team."

Felipe, who was fifty-eight at the time, hailed from the Dominican Republic, and his broken English, coupled with the fact that he had a moustache that obscured his mouth, and occasionally looked down or away from people he was addressing, made it difficult for me to understand everything he said.

Afraid of starting my big-league career by creating the impression I would be difficult to manage, I nodded at everything he said, even if I didn't quite understand it. Maybe it was that extra sense I've always believed I possess kicking in again, but I had no trouble making out the words that mattered most to me.

"Be ready to play," Felipe told me.

To get ready, I was escorted by a clubhouse attendant, who walked me past an unlimited supply of candy bars, sunflower seeds, and bubble gum, to a locker, where a jersey, with *16* and the name *Pride* stitched across the back, was waiting for me.

I was awestruck by the whole atmosphere, and I couldn't believe I was going to play with many of the players I had been watching for years. Some of the veterans were gracious enough to act as if they were inspired by me, too. It was not uncommon for veterans to shun rookies, but this time the veterans immediately tried to make me feel welcome.

Before I could pull up the chair in front of my locker and change into my first big-league uniform, some of the Expos' biggest stars reached out to me.

"Welcome to the Expos," Marquis Grissom said as he shook my hand. "I know all about you and I'm impressed with what you have accomplished."

Other veterans, like Larry Walker and Delino DeShields, offered up similar sentiments. They treated me like I was already one of the guys, and I really appreciated that. But inside, I didn't feel like one of the guys. Not yet, anyway. Since I joined my first T-ball team, my goal had always been to fit in with others and prove I belonged. I always loved being around people, and more than anything, I wanted people to love being around me, too.

But I hadn't yet contributed to my new team, so I didn't yet feel like one of them. The Expos were trying to chase down the Philadelphia Phillies in the National League's East Division, and they had no room for excess baggage as they fought for a pennant.

I wasn't really thinking about the pennant race at that point. I was just too busy thinking about how I would do, and how I could help.

I didn't do anything that first day except sit and wait. While the Expos defeated Cincinnati, 4–2, I sat in the dugout, taking in the surreal surroundings of my new home. With its Kevlar dome, artificial-turf infield, and drab concrete exterior, Montreal's Olympic Stadium felt more like a bunker than a ballpark. Originally built to host the 1976 Summer Olympics, "The Big O," as it was known, had been plagued by budget overruns. The original projected cost of $120 million ballooned to $770 million when it opened for the '76 Olympics, and that was before the costly and dysfunctional retractable dome was added.

Perhaps because I was hurtling toward a strange, new world at breakneck speed, with no idea what I'd find, and no way of knowing if I'd be able to survive, I thought the stadium felt like a spaceship and I was an alien from another planet.

After feasting on a postgame spread, which was prepared by the Expos clubhouse chef, I didn't have a chance to come back down to earth. The Expos checked me into the posh Queen Elizabeth Hotel and told me they'd foot the bill for my first seven days in Montreal.

The Queen Elizabeth is a stately and elegant hotel located in downtown Montreal. The property gained notoriety when John Lennon and Yoko Ono staged their bed-in there and recorded "Give Peace a Chance" in room 1742, on June 1, 1969. Although I, of course, had heard of Lennon, I'd never listened to his music, and didn't really have much of a frame of reference for the former Beatle's profound impact on popular culture.

Queen Elizabeth II had stayed at the hotel, too, and I was feeling like royalty myself. The accommodations were a world apart from the fleabag motor lodges I had stayed in while playing in the low minor leagues, and a huge upgrade from the Rochester Holiday Inn I had slept in two nights earlier. Mike Quade was right: I had been summoned to paradise. But I still felt like I hadn't done anything to deserve such regal treatment.

Exhausted from the all-night bus ride and emotionally spent from my first day in a big-league uniform, I was terrified that I might oversleep and miss the game the next afternoon. So I stopped by the front desk, introduced myself as the Expos' newest player, and put the five-star hotel's staff to work.

"I'm deaf and I forgot to bring my vibrating alarm clock," I explained, "and I can't be late for tomorrow's game. Can you make sure I don't oversleep?" Oversleeping had long been one of my biggest professional and personal fears, the one thing my other senses couldn't compensate for.

Excited, but nervous and alone, I retreated to the ornate surroundings of my room. There I called my best friend from high school, Steve Grupe, who was working at Lockheed Martin in Washington, DC, and invited him to come up for a game. I wanted to share the moment and figured Steve's presence would help me feel more at home.

Then I pulled the pillowy down comforter up over my shoulders, curled up, and ended a dreamlike day by dreaming I'd be able to make a good impression on the Expos before I made a bad one. With the curtains still drawn, the lights and the TV all turned off, my dreams were abruptly interrupted. I was sound asleep, and then suddenly I woke up and saw a shadowy figure at the end of my bed, wiggling my toes. I leapt out of bed, still unsure of whether what was happening was real or a dream. It turned out to be a major-league, wiggly-toe wake-up call.

It was an elderly man, dressed in a full bellman's outfit, the little hat and everything, and he had his hands on my toes. He was wiggling them, saying, "Good morning, Mr. Pride, time to wake up!"

I jumped up and asked him what he was doing, and he told me he had been instructed to enter my room because I couldn't hear him knocking on the door. Then he walked across the room, pulled the blinds open, and said, "Is there anything else I can do for you, Mr. Pride?"

Needless to say, I just tipped him and showed him the door. Then I showered and made the ten-minute drive back to Olympic Stadium, where the start of my major-league career continued to slumber without a wake-up call from Alou. I sat on the bench again, failing to make it into the Expos' 3–2 win over the Reds. We then left immediately after the game for a three-game series in St. Louis.

On the team plane I wanted to fit in, but was too nervous to join the veterans who were playing cards. Instead, I buckled my seat belt, placed my seat and tray table in the upright position, and folded my hands across my lap, unaware that FAA rules don't necessarily apply to charter flights, where virtually no one remains stationary for long. Some of the players got a chuckle out of the uptight rookie, and it occurred to me that I might be trying too hard.

In St. Louis the Cardinals' legendary play-by-play announcer, Jack Buck, singled me out for a pregame interview, a rare honor for a September call-up. I was happy to oblige, and Mr. Buck was wonderful, but I was mostly unaware of his legendary status because I had never heard his work on the radio.

When I'm playing, my own play-by-play runs through my head. Whether it sounds anything like Buck, or Vin Scully, or any other titan of baseball broadcasting, is impossible for me to know. To me, the sounds of the game exist only inside my head.

Later that same night, I got my first major-league at bat, facing Todd Burns as a pinch hitter. I swung at Burns's first pitch, flying out to center field. When we got back to the team hotel, I called my father in Maryland.

"Dad," I said, "I can hit major-league pitching."

When we returned to Montreal, we hosted Philadelphia in a pivotal three-game series. The Expos trailed the Phillies by five games entering the series, but had been closing fast, picking up four-and-a-half games in the month of September. Philadelphia broke out to a 7–3 lead in the first game, before we came storming back in the seventh inning. With two men on, our pitcher Chris Nabholz was due up.

"Get ready," Montreal bench coach Tim Johnson told me, and my heart began beating faster as I grabbed my bat, donned a helmet, and retreated to a tunnel beneath the stands. There I placed a ball on a tee, took a swing to loosen up, and was overcome with a sense of *déjà* vu. This, I realized, was a lot like the feeling I had before my first T-ball game, when, as a six-year-old, I wanted to prove that I belonged, have a little fun, and follow my dream, just like everyone else. Nothing had changed, and everything had changed.

"Now hitting for Nabholz, number sixteen, Curtis Pride," the public-address announcer blared, but all I heard was the sound of my own voice inside my head, running my own play-by-play and offering up instructions.

Be aggressive, my inner voice kept telling me as I walked into the batter's box to face Philadelphia's Bobby Thigpen. *If you get a fastball, go after it. You can hit up here. Be aggressive.*

On his first offering, Thigpen gave me the fastball I was looking for. I got good wood on the ball, and it jumped off my bat, a screaming liner toward the gap between the outfielders in deep-left center field. The ball caromed off the padded outfield wall for a double, scoring two runs, and bringing the Expos to within a run, at 7–6. *Huge.* I would go on to score the tying run, and we eventually won the game, 8–7.

After running to second base for a stand-up double, I then stood on the bag, the Olympic Stadium faithful standing right along with me. Many of those in the sellout crowd that night were aware that I was deaf because of a feature story about me that had been published in the Montreal newspaper earlier that week.

The crowd's uproar continued to grow louder and louder, but I didn't notice. I had always been an aggressive base runner, and I was too busy thinking about stealing third base to notice anything else. When Phillies manager Jim Fregosi summoned Larry Anderson from the bullpen to replace Thigpen, the crowd used the break in the game from the pitching change to continue standing and cheering, but I still didn't notice.

"If they had one of those meters where they measure the decibel level," Jerry Manuel, Montreal's third-base coach that night, told me, "it would have been off the charts."

Jerry later remarked that he got chills all over his body. So did my best friend, Steve, who had traveled to Montreal to watch me play big-league ball for the first time. Directly behind home plate, Jim Tracy, my Double-A manager, stood and joined in the ovation. Jim told me in the clubhouse after the game that I was a hero to him because I set out to do something that a lot of people didn't think was possible. "When you did it," he told me, "I got goose bumps."

It gave me great satisfaction that Jim was at the game, because, as I mentioned, his tutelage earlier that year in Harrisburg had helped to restore my confidence, putting me back on course for the big leagues. The ballpark was filled with a mostly white, predominantly French-Canadian crowd that night. Just days earlier, most of the fans in attendance had never even heard of me. I was a young African American whose minor-league exploits had largely gone unnoticed. But word had spread quickly there was something unique about me, and the Montreal fans were responding to me as one of their own.

Three days later, these same fans, many of them teary-eyed, would tell me how much the moment meant to them when, as a guest on Mitch Melnick's talk show on the Expos' flagship radio station, I answered questions relayed to me by Mitch.

With the Phillies' new pitcher warming up, Jerry Manuel had time to walk from the third-base coaching box onto the field and toward me. "Do I have the green light to steal?" I asked. But Jerry didn't answer. Instead, he pointed at my helmet, so I thought there was something on it. I wondered if I needed to get a new one.

He shook his head. "No," he said, "I'm calling you over because they're cheering for you, and they want you to tip your cap." Then Jerry gently put his arm around my shoulder and turned me toward the crowd.

I took my helmet off, and that's when I saw everybody on their feet cheering, although I still didn't quite know what it was all about.

Then Jerry told me. "It's for you."

I looked up and did a slow panorama of the stadium's three decks, scanning the sellout crowd that stood as one. Now I had chills, just like everyone else. Although I loved poker, I had always had a lousy poker face. There were a lot of times when I couldn't stop smiling, but this was not one of them.

Keep a straight face, I kept telling myself, as if I were holding a royal flush, instead of a batting helmet. *Don't smile.*

I wanted the baseball world to know this wasn't a onetime shot, that there would be more hits, that I was merely doing what I expected of myself. If I smiled, I feared, it might send a message that I believed I had gotten my one shot and I was done, that I was some sort of novelty act. I wanted everyone to know I was merely another ballplayer recording his first major-league hit, and there would be plenty more to come.

Finally second-base umpire Gary Darling walked over. "Smile," he told me. "Smile!"

Only then did I give in, waving my helmet to the crowd. As I stood on second base, a wide smile lighting up my face, tears welling up in my eyes, I thought about how hard I had worked, and how much I had accomplished. I also thought how proud my parents would be, and how close I had come to quitting baseball a year earlier.

People had always written me off, I thought. *I was always the underdog. Sometimes I felt like I had to work harder than everyone else, just to be taken seriously. This moment makes everything I went through worth it.*

Mike Lansing stepped into the batter's box, and Anderson threw him a pitch, but no one noticed. All eyes, many of them damp, remained on me as I took an aggressive lead off second base. The cheering persisted. By now, the ovation had gone on for so long and gotten so rambunctious, I was feeling it. The turbulence from the noise echoed off the inside of the stadium's concrete walls and Kevlar dome, reverberating back down through the playing surface, where it created a vibration that shook me to my core.

"It was," Jerry Manuel told me, "one of the most incredible moments I've ever seen. The crowd was so loud that it was almost as if they were trying to make you hear. They knew you couldn't, but they were going to the next level to do everything they could to make you hear."

But, other than a faint, distorted noise that was amplified through the hearing aid in my left ear, I never heard the cheers of the crowd as they saluted me for the very same reason the kids on the playground used to make fun of me.

As I stood alone in silence, while 45,757 fans at Montreal's Olympic Stadium screamed their lungs out, I began to understand that while my disability robbed me of my hearing, it gave me a voice. Deafness—the very thing that once made me feel alone and isolated—was in reality a gift that enabled me to connect with people in a way that would not be possible if I could hear.

CHAPTER 13

The Story of Our Lives

After that big hit in Montreal, I got letters from deaf children so often, I was no longer surprised when a trainer or public relations person would drop the correspondence off in my locker, frequently many at a time. I'd sort through them, marvel at the stories of courage and bravery from kids dealing with everything from deafness to blindness to debilitating illnesses or injuries. Then I would answer them, one by one, including a personal note of encouragement. I wanted those kids to find the success I was enjoying in baseball, and I wanted them to have the role model I never had.

What turned out to be the most significant letter I ever received was delivered to me at the Expos Spring Training facility in West Palm Beach, Florida. Like so many others, it came from a deaf child, but this letter was different. Usually, I got that kind of letter and I hoped I would be able, in some small way, to change the life of the person who wrote it.

This one would change the life of the person who received it, in ways I never could have imagined.

Justin Drezner was an ambitious eleven-year-old from New Jersey, who could not hear, but he didn't want his deafness to stop him from envisioning an unlimited future for himself. He was determined to make the most of his fifth-grade assignment to write a paper about his role model. Because Justin and I both have a hearing disability, he chose to write a paper about me, and he wanted to know if I would meet him for a face-to-face interview.

Of course, I would.

Interactions like this were one of the reasons I wanted to play professional baseball. I loved proving that a deaf person could compete on equal footing, without being considered a charity case, and I typically took a certain unique satisfaction in proving the naysayers wrong. When it came to encouraging kids like Justin—kids like me—there was a sense of pure joy. There was personal satisfaction in seeing the hope in the eyes of a young boy or girl, and even more at seeing the happiness on the faces of their parents when I was meeting with their son or daughter. It gave me a purpose I couldn't find anywhere else.

I had been Justin and all the others, and while I hated being different and being singled out, deep down I always knew there was cause for optimism. Maybe it was the magic of youth, and perhaps I was just naive to believe I could overcome my deafness. However, there was always a part of me that was hopeful. Maybe it was something primal, a survival instinct perhaps, that told me I had to believe because there would always be others who didn't, and I had to compensate for them. While my parents were always outwardly encouraging, when I saw the uncertainty on the faces of other deaf kids and their parents, it made me wonder if my own parents secretly had their doubts about me. I suspect they did.

When I met with a deaf child, I actually got almost as much from their parents as I did from the kids themselves. The wonder and optimism of those parents and family members reflected on me and I always left those encounters feeling exhilarated, like my own future had opened up to the limitless possibilities of youth.

It wasn't uncommon for these sessions to result in tears, and often they were my own. I'd buck up, put on my game face for our interactions, then go back to my locker and wonder if I had done enough, if I had dispensed the right dose of optimism to compensate for the negativity those kids got on the playgrounds and ball fields. Sometimes, after the meetings, I would get emotional and not know why. Were these feelings of wonder at being the one chosen to help these kids? Or were they feelings of despair, brought on by the unfairness of it all, the thought of these kids going through the same abuse I had faced? I wasn't entirely sure, but I knew I wanted to help them, and I wanted to show their parents an example of a self-sufficient professional baseball player who happened to be deaf.

Justin's letter detailed how Spring Training coincided with his spring break from school, and that he would be in Florida with his parents. I responded by telling him if he could make it to West Palm Beach Municipal Stadium, I would be happy to meet with him. It was impossible not to see a little of myself in Justin.

Like the other children I met with, Justin arrived at the appointed time with supportive parents in tow, but on this day there was someone else on hand to witness our introduction. Lisa Matejcik, a TV reporter at the NBC affiliate in West Palm Beach, had gotten wind of the meeting and thought it would make a nice human-interest story. Lisa was doing the story on Justin and me, but I believe the fact that this was the kind of story she wanted to broadcast into the world tells you as much about her as it does me.

Justin and I did a joint interview with Lisa, and it went well. She asked insightful questions and Justin gave heartfelt answers, which is always a great combination. While I was always thrilled to do these pieces, I never knew how they would land. Reporters could sometimes overplay things, making me sound like some sort of savior, or they could be maudlin, making the deaf child an object of pity.

Lisa did neither. She found the perfect tone, bringing us together for a joint interview that showed her audience our obvious connection, without being condescending or overbearing. She was a natural, and I could tell right away that she had an innate ability to relate to people. I was impressed with her capacity to comprehend the humanity of the meeting between Justin and me, and her ability to share it with her audience.

We did the interview, Lisa thanked me for my time, and that was that. We went our separate ways. A couple of weeks later, I injured my hand because of overwork, so when camp broke and the rest of the team went north to Montreal for the start of the season, I stayed behind in West Palm Beach to rehab the injury. In the world of baseball only the strong survive, and if you are not healthy enough to help your team, you get left behind. I was deadweight.

Ordinarily, Florida is one of my favorite places on earth. I love the weather, particularly in the spring, and the swaying palm trees always put me in a good mood, as if I have found my own magical paradise of sunshine and baseball. But with the other Expos players gone, my happy place began to depress me.

I was forced to stay behind for five weeks, and the days soon grew long and lonely. I'd do my rehab in the morning, but then, unable to take batting practice or engage in any baseball-related activities, the days would drag on. And on . . . and on . . .

My roommate at the time was Derek Aucoin, a relief pitcher, who was also left back on rehab assignment, and we would spend our time sitting around the apartment we shared, watching TV and counting the days until we could go north and rejoin the Expos. Then Derek got an idea. Why not take our bikes for a ride along Palm Beach? It would get us out of the house and the activity would be good for us.

Later that day, as we were riding our bicycles along a bike path, I noticed Lisa, who was Rollerblading on the same trail. It was hard not to notice Lisa. Derek couldn't believe it when I told him I knew her, and he wanted me to be his wingman. It was funny, on the mound Derek was a closer, but out here, in the real world, he wanted me to help him with an introduction to Lisa.

It was about three weeks after our interview, and I kind of liked the fact that Derek was interested in Lisa because it meant I could approach her without any pressure. I would be doing a friend a favor, not putting myself on the line. Then, after being around me, maybe Lisa would fall hard—for me. That was my hope, anyway.

Still, I wasn't sure if Lisa would remember me, so it took Derek's nonstop urging for me to approach her. Finally I did, and she remembered me immediately.

Was she busy?

Did she have plans for the afternoon?

Would she like to join us for happy hour?

"Sure," she said.

"Great!" I replied enthusiastically.

Then she said, "As long as my fiancé can come along."

Derek was crushed.

So was I, of course, but I did a good job of keeping that to myself.

Lisa was off the market, but I had felt such a strong connection to her during our interview, I still wanted to go out with her and her fiancé. She was the kind of person I wanted to know better, even if there was no chance of it leading to anything between us more than a platonic friendship.

We met up at E.R. Bradley's Saloon, a popular bar. Lisa's fiancé was from Maryland, which gave us something in common, and I liked him right away. Despite Derek's broken heart, and my secret disappointment, we all had a nice night out and promised to keep in touch.

Soon after, my injured hand got better, and I went back to Ottawa. Because of the delayed start to my season, I spent the rest of that time back in Triple-A Ottawa, and then, after playing in the Arizona Fall League that October, my dad flew with me down to Florida to help me look for a condo. I knew I would likely be spending every Spring Training in Florida, and buying a place there made financial sense.

During our house hunt I called Lisa and invited her and her fiancé to join us for dinner at a local barbecue place. Lisa showed up at the restaurant alone, and when she told me they had broken things off, my heart soared. No fiancé and no Derek. This was a fastball, right in my wheelhouse. We had dinner with my father, and then I asked her out.

Lisa and I had immediate chemistry, no doubt because we had so much in common. Lisa had played softball for one year at the University of Dayton, before transferring to Central Florida to major in journalism, and she loved baseball. She grew up in Ohio as a big Cleveland Indians fan and knew the game as well as I did. As a player herself, she understood what it was like to have so much of yourself invested in a game, and as a lifetime fan of Ohio State football, she understood there were times when the world stopped, and a game played by others became the most important thing in the universe. When we watched baseball games together, she understood the nuance of the game and loved it as much as I did.

Like me, Lisa was very active; she loved the outdoors and enjoyed going fishing. As our relationship continued to grow, I began to think that Lisa might be that special someone for the rest of my life. Wanting to do something special, I invited her to join me on a fishing trip at Lake Cabonga, about two hundred miles north of Montreal.

Lake Cabonga is isolated and unspoiled, just pure blue water, green shorelines, and the kind of fishing you dream about. It is one of the most beautiful places I have ever fished at, and, with Lisa along on the trip, it felt like heaven on earth. We rented a pontoon boat, and we caught a huge haul of walleye in what was easily my best fishing day ever. I didn't want our time together to end.

There was only one thing to do. I took her fishing pole to bait her hook, and when she wasn't looking, I put an engagement ring (an inexpensive stand-in ring) on the hook. Then I cast it out for her, in more ways than one. I handed her the pole, and before long, she got a bite. She reeled it in, and my heart fluttered. Facing an All-Star big-league pitcher was nothing compared to this.

"Did you get it?" I asked.

"I think I lost my bait," she said.

My heart pounded harder. *Please, no,* I thought. *Just let her find the ring on the end of her line. Let this be a story I tell our grandkids, not one I recount in therapy.*

Then she looked at her line and said, "I think I have something on my hook."

I moved closer, inspecting the hook.

"What is it?" I asked.

"I think it's a ring," she said.

Then I got down on my knees and formally proposed. She accepted, thank God, no psychological damage done. It was the moment I had hoped for, the one I had planned for.

We got engaged in 1997, and then we got married—twice. I would do it all over again a third time, too. I have had much good fortune in my lifetime, met a lot of wonderful people, and been to many amazing places, but none has had a greater impact on my life than the day I crossed paths with Lisa for an interview on a Florida baseball field during Spring Training.

It was always our dream to get married in Hawaii. Maui was gorgeous, unspoiled, and romantic. It had endless days of sunshine, a wide array of outdoor activities, and fantastic fishing. We thought a destination wedding in Hawaii would be the perfect place to start our life together, but we didn't want to burden our friends and family members with the expense of a trip.

Lisa and I were beginning our life as a married couple, but family was our top priority, so we were determined to have a ceremony that honored our parents, grandparents, and siblings. No way would either one of us be getting married without our family as a primary part of the wedding.

We found a way to have our cake and eat it, too. We decided to elope to Hawaii, then followed it up with a more formal ceremony in Florida, where our families could be part of it. Lisa is Catholic and always wanted to be married in the Catholic Church, and we wanted our marriage to be a sacrament under God. As of 2024, Lisa and I have been married for twenty-six years and have two beautiful children—Noelle, age twenty, and Colten, who is seventeen. I feel blessed every day to have such a fantastic wife and terrific family.

CHAPTER 14

Big-League Glory, Big-Time Disappointment

Imagine having all your dreams come true, seeing a lifetime of hard work pay off and feeling pure exhilaration as you are celebrated by a stadium full of adoring fans. Then picture it all being taken away during a five-minute meeting, or a phone call from a baseball executive or your agent.

Those are the typical bookends of a Major League Baseball career, and—except for a small percentage of players—you can't have one without the other. One day you're on top of the world; the next day it feels like the weight of the world is on top of you. It was an emotional swing I would experience, over and over, during my playing career.

When I made my big-league debut with Montreal in 1993, I believed I had made a breakthrough. I thought I could be an Expo for life. However, that initial shot of adrenaline and glory in Montreal, at the end of the '93 season, was followed by more time at Triple-A Ottawa, and a brief rehab stint at Single-A West Palm Beach, and then an unremarkable return to the Expos in 1995, where I hit just .175 in forty-eight games.

Two years, and fifty-eight big-league games after my big breakthrough, I realized my time in Montreal would just last a short time. But it turned out that I wasn't entirely done with Montreal (I returned to play thirty-six more games for the Expos in 2001), but I couldn't have known that at the time.

What I did know is that the Expos did not tender me a contract after the '95 season. I thought maybe my career had reached a dead end, but it turned out to only be a slight detour. I was about to become a baseball journeyman, which was fine by me. I had a bat, a glove, and a pair of spikes, and I would gladly go anywhere to keep playing. Being "non-tendered" by the Expos was an eye-opener. It made me realize my career in the big leagues was not guaranteed and I needed to make the most of what time remained.

At the same time I began to realize the power of Major League Baseball. In nearly every city I visited, a writer or TV reporter wanted to do a story on my deafness, and it began to dawn on me that if I was more proactive, I could reach many deaf and hard-of-hearing kids looking for a positive role model.

My agent at the time was Ron Shapiro, a wonderful man who always looked out for my best interests. But Ron also represented Hall of Famers Cal Ripken Jr., Kirby Puckett, Eddie Murray, and Brooks Robinson, so his plate was full. My father and I decided to go agent shopping. We wanted to work with someone in the greater Washington, DC, area who could also arrange speaking engagements and get me in front of deaf and hard-of-hearing kids whenever possible.

We decided on Len Elmore, a former University of Maryland basketball star and NBA player, who had been working in broadcasting. Elmore was embarking on a career as a sports agent, and his firm, Precept Sports and Entertainment, had gotten off to a strong start, signing, in its first year, NBA basketball players Walt Williams, of Maryland, and Harold Miner, of the University of Southern California, both first-round lottery picks. Sam Cassell, of Florida State, and Terry Dehere, of Seton Hall, soon followed, and by the time Precept Sports signed Joe Smith, the first overall pick in the 1995 NBA Draft, they had an impressive roster of clients.

When my parents and I went to our initial meeting at Mr. Elmore's office in Columbia, Maryland, a significant portion of the presentation was made by Joe Strasser, who also worked in their office. Joe had an undergraduate degree from Ohio University. He had also decided to get a JD degree from the University of Denver's College of Law, which at the time was one of the few law schools in the country that offered a specific course in sports law.

After obtaining his law degree, Joe received a coveted judicial clerkship with Judge Ferdinand Fernandez at the U.S. District Court in Los Angeles, and then joined the Washington, DC, office of the prestigious New York–based law firm Debevoise & Plimpton, where he specialized in large cases involving the federal securities laws. But the business of professional sports was Joe's first love, so he left the day-to-day practice of law to join Precept Sports as their general counsel and director of player contracts.

During our meeting Joe had promised me and my parents that he would work hard to extend my public profile and reach more of the Deaf community. Shortly after I signed with Precept, Joe somehow convinced CBS's *48 Hours*, hosted by Dan Rather, to come down to Spring Training in Lakeland, Florida, and document my attempt to make the opening-day roster of the Detroit Tigers.

Dan Rather did a great job on the piece, which was broadcast nationwide, and it had an especially powerful ending, with manager Buddy Bell informing me I had made the Tigers team. I was impressed that Joe had lined up such a legendary broadcaster to do a story on me, and from that moment on, my relationship with Joe grew closer and closer, to the point where I now consider him to be an extended part of my family.

During that season with the Tigers, whenever I would call in to the Precept office on the TTY relay machine, Mr. Elmore always seemed to be on another call with one of his basketball clients, or so I was told, and the receptionist would transfer me to Joe. After several of those calls, and the comfort level I was developing with Joe, I stopped even asking for Len and just asked the receptionist to be connected directly to Joe.

Joe's credentials are impeccable, and he has always been

straightforward with me in our business dealings, but what really sealed our relationship were a lot of late-night phone calls. During road trips it wasn't uncommon for me to return to the team hotel, full of excitement and adrenaline, unable to sleep after a game, and I would often call Joe.

Those were the days before cell phones, and the fine art of texting leveled the field for deaf people, which meant that a simple phone call with me required a complex communiqué akin to being translated at the United Nations. With a TTY machine I could conduct a phone call with a hearing person, which was great, except for one thing: The person on the other end had to have one of the costly devices and have the patience to carry on a conversation through a machine. To my good fortune Joe invested in a TTY machine and exhibited remarkable equanimity in dealing with me.

At all hours of the night, Joe and I would talk on the TTY machine. We usually started with that night's game and the business of baseball, but then would also invariably proceed to current events, popular books and movies, and many other subjects. I felt like I had found a kindred spirit. It wasn't until much later in our dealings that Joe shared something with me that helped me understand why he was so comfortable around me, why he treated me like a brother.

A few years before Joe was born, his own brother Thomas, who had been given the nickname of Binky or Bink as a young child, was diagnosed with syringomyelia, an extremely rare disease that causes a fluid-filled cavity in the spinal cord that slowly renders its victim physically incapacitated. Bink, the oldest of the five boys that made up the Strasser clan, was in grade school when he was first stricken, and, gradually, went from walking with crutches to being bedridden, to becoming almost totally paralyzed. Joe, the youngest in the Strasser family, was just a young child and then a teenager as he helplessly watched Bink struggle with the incurable disease.

Like Joe, Bink loved sports, and watching games on television became a great escape from the ravages of his illness. Joe would frequently forgo the carefree activities his friends were engaged in, instead spending time with his ailing brother watching baseball and other sports on TV. Many times Joe and Bink would even keep a play-by-play record of the baseball games they watched together in scorebooks they obtained from their local sporting-goods store in Tiffin, Ohio.

Bink passed away too soon, at the age of thirty-two, when Joe was just a sophomore in high school. I suspect that experience had a lasting impact on Joe, leaving him more compassionate, more tolerant, and, most of all, more comfortable in his interactions with someone who has a disability.

Whatever the impact Bink had on Joe, I have been one of the prime beneficiaries. While I never met Bink, it's clear he left an impression on Joe, changing the course of his life and, in turn, making an important impact on my life and career, long after Bink himself passed from this earth. It's a story that reminds me of the importance of making the most of our time here, impacting as many people as we can in the belief that they will find a way to pass it on.

Bink gave something to Joe, who gave it to me. I am honored to share that gift of his, along with my own personal insight and experiences.

CHAPTER 15

Glory Days

I spent the summer of '96 in Detroit, and it was there, playing in historic Tiger Stadium, that I had my best season in Major League Baseball. I hit .300 and was still young and naive enough to believe I would be a mainstay in the Tigers' outfield for the next decade. A year later, though, I was out of the organization.

It was heartbreaking, but in retrospect it had been one of the most important experiences of my career. My time with the Tigers showed other teams that I could play at the big-league level on a consistent basis, and other teams were interested in signing me because I proved I could play at that level. The Detroit manager, Buddy Bell, gave me an opportunity and treated me well. Looking back, I choose to accentuate the positive, something I have always preached.

Hitting an even .300 in 267 at bats for the Tigers during that '96 campaign remains one of the greatest accomplishments of my career. In my last at bat of the season, I needed a hit to finish with a .300 average for the year. I would love to tell you I had no idea of what I was hitting and that I did not know a .300 batting average hung in the balance, but as I stepped to the plate, I knew exactly what was at stake.

I hit a hard grounder to the hole at second base, where Fernando Viña, of the Milwaukee Brewers, made a nice diving stop. He got up and threw to first. My speed never paid bigger dividends than at that moment, as I beat his throw by a fraction of a second. As I stood on first base, I didn't know if the official scorer would rule a hit or an error. It could have gone either way, and I was praying for a hit. When the scoreboard flashed *H*, I tried to pretend like I didn't notice, but deep down I was thrilled and relieved.

The Tigers then signed me to another contract for the '97 season, and I went to Spring Training excited and ready to build on my excellent season as the Tigers starting left fielder or designated hitter against right-handed pitchers. Other than the .320 batting average of All-Star Bobby Higginson, my .300 batting average in 1996 was the second best on the team, and higher than even those of long-established Tigers regulars Travis Fryman, Cecil Fielder, and Tony Clark.

My excitement was short-lived, however, as during Spring Training a young prospect, Bubba Trammell, was given most of the playing time in left field. Bubba had an excellent '96 season, where he hit .316 in 134 games between Double-A Erie and Triple-A Toledo. He had been drafted by the Tigers in the eleventh round two years before, so he wasn't a high-round draft pick that might normally cause an organization to feature him to its fans.

Coinciding with Bubba's excellent '96 season in the minors was the fact that this year was also the final season played by the Tigers shortstop, and future Hall of Famer, Alan Trammell. Alan played in sixty-six games for the Tigers that season as he was winding down his legendary career, and it was an honor to play on the same team with him.

With the extremely popular Alan Trammell having just retired, a part of me thinks the Tigers were hoping for a public relations benefit from having another Trammell featured on the team the very next season, even though Alan and Bubba are in no way related. When Bubba, a right-handed hitter, was in the starting lineup on opening day, even against a right-handed starting pitcher, my frustration only grew higher.

I was in the starting lineup in only nine of the first twenty games of the season, but still kept my focus and hit an excellent .306 in those thirty-six at bats. Conversely, Bubba was provided fifty at bats in those twenty games and hit .260, which was certainly respectable for a first-year player. As April went into May, and Bubba's average started to decline, reaching a low of .239 on May 7, my playing time not only didn't increase, I began to be utilized even more only as a pinch hitter and late-inning substitute.

My frustration reached its peak in late August, as I was in the starting lineup for only eight games the entire month of July, and only two games the first few weeks of August. I called my father and Joe and they suggested I request a meeting with Randy Smith, who was the Tigers general manager.

I took their advice and made an appointment to see Randy in his office. But when I showed up, Randy was still at home. His assistant said he would meet me later in the day, but instead, he showed up that afternoon in Buddy Bell's office. He called me in and told me I was being sent down to the minors. It came as a complete surprise, as I thought we would be talking about playing time. Instead, he talked and I said nothing.

I called Joe right after that meeting, and he advised me that I had the option of accepting the demotion or exercising my right to become a free agent. I decided my best option was to become a free agent and get a fresh start someplace new. For about one week I was out of baseball, wondering what was going on, what would happen next. I was scared. While Joe was on the phone trying to find the best place for me, I was worried that because it was near the end of the season, nobody would pick me up and my career might come to an unceremonious end.

Soon after, it turned out the best opportunity for me was in Boston. Dan Duquette, the Red Sox general manager, had been with the Expos when I was there, and he liked me. Joe worked out a contract for me to join the Red Sox organization, and I was happy to go to Triple-A Pawtucket. Lisa and I packed up our place in Detroit and drove to Rhode Island, excited to have a fresh start in a new organization.

After a short time playing in a few games in Pawtucket at the end of their season, I got promoted to Boston in September, right at the same time as Jason Varitek, who was my roommate. In Boston, like my historic first hit in Montreal, lightning struck again. In my first at bat for the Red Sox, I crushed a fastball from Chicago White Sox reliever Keith Foulke to dead center field, where it landed on the camera platform high above the famous green wall, easily over four hundred feet from home plate. At that time I became only the seventh player in the over-one-hundred-year history of the storied Red Sox franchise to hit a home run in their first at bat. The fact that it occurred in historic Fenway Park made it even more special—another great memory.

That home run was just a lone bolt of lightning, and there would be no electrical storm. Not for me, not in Boston. I played in just two games for the Red Sox at the end of that season. The next year I was hoping to go back to Boston, but I had shoulder surgery in the off-season, which was performed by Dr. Arthur Pappas, the renowned Red Sox team doctor. The injury was a dislocated shoulder that was the result of diving for a ball in the outfield. It was very painful, but I tried to play through it.

After a few years of professional baseball, I became accustomed to the pain that came with overcoming injuries. In all, I had seven surgeries over the course of my career: one on my left shoulder, two on my right wrist, one each on both knees, one on my left toe, and one on my right elbow. My shoulder rehabilitation, however, would not lead me back to Fenway as the Sox left me off their roster and I found myself looking for a new team again.

I recovered quickly and signed with Atlanta for the 1998 season, where I had one of the best experiences of my career. Under Braves manager Bobby Cox, the team was in the midst of winning a remarkable fourteen consecutive National League Eastern Division titles, a feat unprecedented in any major professional sport. I had the privilege of being part of their eighth consecutive division championship during the 1998 season, playing in seventy games and hitting .252.

Walking into the Braves clubhouse every day was like stepping into a wing of the Hall of Fame, with Bobby Cox, pitchers Greg Maddux, John Smoltz, and Tom Glavine, along with third baseman (and outfielder) Chipper Jones—all destined for Cooperstown. Outfielder Andruw Jones won his first of ten consecutive Gold Gloves that season, and I think Andruw also has a good shot of making it to the Hall of Fame. Yet, for all the star power, the Braves never let individual egos get in the way of winning. We were a team that played together and believed in one another, traits that can be traced back to the leadership of Bobby Cox.

Over the course of his twenty-nine-year managerial career, Bobby Cox was ejected from 161 games, the most ever by a manager, largely because he was so devoted to backing up his players. I believe Bobby was every bit as important to the Braves' success as the Hall of Famers he penciled into the lineup, and he remains my all-time favorite manager. Bobby was a great communicator, and always treated me with the utmost respect and I will always appreciate that.

I clearly remember one of my first days with the Braves. I was in Bobby's office, and he said, "Curtis, on my team I treat everyone the same. Tell me everything I need to know about your deafness and anything I need to be aware of, so it never is an issue between us the rest of the season." I told him that other than remembering that I needed to see his face when he talked to me, he didn't have to worry about anything.

I totally respected Bobby for being so direct, and that season with the Braves turned out to be the season I enjoyed the most of my entire career. Unfortunately, we were not able to reward Bobby, the Braves organization, and the people of Atlanta with a World Series Championship in 1998. After sailing through the regular season with 106 wins, we entered the postseason as heavy favorites to win the World Series. Our "Big 3" starting rotation of Maddux, Smoltz, and Glavine had won a combined fifty-five games during the regular season—with Denny Neagle and Kevin Millwood, the fourth and fifth starters, teaming to win another thirty-three games between them. All told, our five starters alone won eighty-eight games, and we finished eighteen games ahead of the second-place New York Mets.

All that great pitching gave us a feeling of invincibility as we opened the playoffs, and we began by sweeping the Chicago Cubs, three games to none, in the National League Division Series. I was confident that I would achieve my lifelong goal of reaching the World Series, but the San Diego Padres then pulled off one of the biggest upsets in the history of postseason baseball, taking the National League Championship Series (NLCS) from us in six games. Adding even more frustration, the Padres then went on to be swept 4–0 by the Yankees in the 1998 World Series.

After the heartbreak of losing to the Padres in the NLCS, my disappointment doubled when the Braves non-tendered me in the offseason and I became a free agent. Soon thereafter, I signed a Triple-A contract with the Kansas City Royals and reported to their 1999 Spring Training camp feeling I had a legitimate chance to make their major-league opening-day roster. However, within the first two weeks of camp, I felt a significant *pop* in my right wrist while engaging in outfield throwing drills and was diagnosed to have torn the extensor carpi ulnaris tendon in the wrist.

The Royals then released me from my contract later that same day and—to add insult to injury—told me they were not going to pay me the two weeks of salary that's normally required when a player is released during Spring Training. Their argument was that the wrist injury was a preexisting condition that was not disclosed to them during my physical, and therefore voided their obligation to pay the two weeks of salary.

However, that simply was not true. I had slightly sprained the ulnar collateral ligament in my right wrist during the previous season in Atlanta, but had totally recovered from that injury. After having surgery to repair the torn tendon from Kansas City's camp, my physicians told me it was clearly not related to or caused by the ligament sprain in Atlanta. Although the two weeks of Triple-A salary the Royals refused to pay me was not a large amount, I still decided, as a matter of principle, to contest their decision by filing a grievance via the Major League Baseball Players Association.

Joe did a terrific job working with the union's lawyers in preparing the legal briefs and, in what was no doubt a rare occurrence, MLB Commissioner Bud Selig sided with a player over team ownership. He issued a detailed written opinion totally agreeing with my side and ordering the Royals to pay me the two weeks of Spring Training salary.

It felt good to be vindicated in winning the grievance, but the simple truth remained that it took several months of rehab to recover from the surgery to repair the torn tendon, and by that point the 1999 season was almost over. Therefore, toward the end of the season, I decided to join the Nashua Pride of the independent Atlantic League.

That decision turned out to be premature, as it was only three months after my surgery, and I was not even close to being 100 percent recovered. I went only two for thirty-two in the fourteen games I played for Nashua against pitchers I would normally hit with little problem. I was grateful to the management in Nashua for providing me that opportunity, and, as it turns out during the roller-coaster ride of my career, I was able to more than pay them back by having two very productive stints in Nashua during both the 2003 and 2004 seasons.

During the offseason between 1999 and 2000, I worked hard to recover fully from the wrist surgery. At age thirty-one, I was convinced I had more baseball left in my body and I was determined to get back to the big leagues. In the spring of 2000, I signed a contract with the New York Mets (ironically, the team that had initially drafted me fourteen years before) and began the season with their Triple-A team in Norfolk, Virginia. I hit the ground running in Norfolk, hitting .290 in my first fifteen games with eleven walks, for an OBP of .488 and OPS of 1.069.

In Triple-A, however, organizations must always balance the goals of winning while also developing their young prospects for future success, and that season the Mets had several prospects in Norfolk that needed regular playing time. So even though I was off to a fast start, manager John Gibbons couldn't get me into the lineup every day. I talked it over with the Mets minor-league front office and they graciously agreed to trade me to the Boston Red Sox, the team I had been with for a brief cup of coffee just three years before.

During my fast start in Norfolk, Joe had heard rumors that a team in the Japanese Professional League was interested in me. So going to Boston also made sense because at that time the leading broker for negotiating with Japanese teams was Ray Poitevint, who was the executive director of international operations for the Red Sox. Ray had developed strong relationships with the decision makers for the Japanese teams, and it was widely known that, along with a player's U.S. agent, Ray was the guy to work with for a possible deal in Japan.

The Red Sox put me in Triple-A Pawtucket to continue to build on what I had been doing in Norfolk and I came through with flying colors. I hit .305 in forty-eight games for Pawtucket, with thirty-eight walks, plus twelve stolen bases, for an OBP of .441 and OPS of 1.012.

With my two-month run of good games in Pawtucket, the Red Sox gave me The Call to the majors in mid-June. I arrived in Boston full of confidence and excited that I could have an excellent chance to get my career back on track to the levels I had reached in Detroit and Atlanta.

CHAPTER 16

It's Not All Glory

My second stint with the Red Sox lasted all of nine games: just long enough for me to endure the only on-the-field controversy of my baseball career related to my deafness. We were in Toronto for a series against the Blue Jays, and the Sunday afternoon game had more than usual pregame attention because the starting pitcher matchup featured our Cy Young winner, and future Hall of Famer, Pedro Martinez, versus the Blue Jays young star and future Cy Young winner, Chris Carpenter.

I played the entire game in left field and, ironically, had an excellent day at the plate getting hits in each of my first three at bats (a double and two singles).

The game was tight throughout and went into extra innings, tied 5–5. In the bottom of the thirteenth inning, we retired the first two Blue Jays batters, and then Chris Woodward hit a high fly ball into the gap to the left-field side of center field. I immediately saw that Carl Everett, our center fielder, was tracking the ball well to be able to make the catch, so as all corner outfielders are trained to do with a ball in the gap in that situation, I ran in a path that would take me well behind Carl to back up the play. However, in the instant right before the ball arrived to Carl, for what would have been a relatively easy catch, he apparently noticed me out of the corner of his eye and flinched. The ball deflected off his glove and rolled away, with Woodward making it all the way to third for a three-base error.

Instead of the inning being over and us getting ready to bat in the top of the fourteenth, the Blue Jays had the potential winning run on third base, with two outs. As fate would have it, the next batter, Tony Batista, singled to right field, giving the Blue Jays a dramatic 6–5 walk-off win.

In the clubhouse reporters gathered around my locker, demanding to know what happened. Had I called for the ball? Did I cost us the game? I patiently explained that no, I had not called for the ball. I was doing what every left fielder is supposed to do in that situation—run in a path behind the other fielder to provide backup.

To his credit, Carl Everett immediately came over, stopped the questions, and said very emphatically, "I didn't catch a ball I should have caught." Then realizing that the reporters still wanted to focus on my deafness, Carl continued to set the record straight. "There's no reason to go any deeper than what I've already said." I will always appreciate Carl being such a stand-up guy and taking up for me when it would have been easier to deflect some of the attention back on me.

Unfortunately, the statements to the media by Red Sox manager Jimy Williams weren't as clear as Carl's. Jimy said he felt there was a "human element" involved in the play, which I think the media then interpreted to mean that one of the two players was deaf, and the other wasn't.

Regardless of how one may or may not interpret what happened on that play in Toronto, about one week later, the Red Sox picked up outfielder Bernard Gilkey on waivers and Jimy called me into his office and told me I was being sent back down to Triple-A. I couldn't help but think the play in Toronto had an impact on that decision.

Plus, my demotion was doubly shocking to me because of something that had occurred a few days after the play in Toronto and before Bernard Gilkey joined the team. We were in Chicago playing the White Sox, and our rookie outfielder, Israel Alcantara, was playing right field. On two different plays during the game, he let fly balls drop in front of him due to lack of hustle, and then late in the game, while running the bases, he got caught between second and third and simply stopped, letting himself easily be tagged out.

Jimy Williams was so angry he went on a loud tirade in the clubhouse. After yelling at the team for several minutes, he told the media in his office that "Israel Alcantara will never play baseball for me again." But when it came time to clear a roster spot a few days later, the Red Sox front office conveniently ignored Israel's lack of hustle and what Williams had previously said. I got sent down, instead, even though I was playing well and had far more big-league experience. Although Alcantara did eventually play in a few more games for the Red Sox later that season, he is now most widely remembered for intentionally and violently drop-kicking a catcher in the face with his metal spikes in a Triple-A game the following season. His entire major-league career consisted of only fifty-two games and ended in 2002, long before I retired in 2008.

Additionally, what made my demotion from Boston even more frustrating, as I referenced earlier, is part of the reason why I signed with Boston, and went to their Triple-A team in Pawtucket—because of the possibility of parlaying that into a contract to play in Japan. While I was in Pawtucket, the Orix BlueWave had indicated they were interested in signing me. But then my promotion to Boston put that possibility on hold. It would, of course, be crazy for any player to put Japan ahead of being on a major-league roster. Still, playing for the Orix BlueWave had its appeal. A stint in Japan would be a cultural experience like no other, combining baseball with travel, meeting new people, and unparalleled adventure. It was a chance to experience all the things I love in a unique setting.

By the time I had spent that short period in Boston, the Orix team in Japan had decided to go in a different direction. All of this left an especially bad taste in my mouth, so I refused the assignment back to Pawtucket and signed a contract with the Los Angeles Dodgers Triple-A affiliate in Albuquerque, New Mexico, instead. Kevin Malone, the Dodgers general manager, had been the director of scouting for the Expos when I got my first major-league hit there in 1993, and he had always liked my game.

There was only a little over one month left in the Triple-A season when I arrived in Albuquerque, but I did well there, hitting .293 in thirty-eight games with an OPS of .909. I didn't get called up to Los Angeles at the end of the Albuquerque season, but I am still grateful to Kevin for giving me the opportunity to finish my season there after what had happened in Boston. I enjoyed my time in New Mexico. It was an especially hot summer, but Albuquerque is a beautiful city. The air is clear and the vistas, especially the Sandia Mountains, were breathtaking.

While I'm still sorry that I missed out on playing in Japan, I did spend a short time playing winter ball in Caracas, Venezuela, after being released by the Expos after the 1995 season. While I was playing for the Caracas Leones, I lived at the Anauco Hilton downtown, which was nice and safe. But it didn't always feel as safe at the stadium.

To say that the fans in Venezuela are passionate about baseball is an understatement. One night in a close and hotly contested game, several fans jumped over the railings and began running at us on the field. Our manager started screaming at us, "Get in the dugout!"

Many other fans were putting their faces against the restraining fence, screaming in Spanish. I had no idea what they were saying. I'm an excellent lip-reader, but it must be in English. Then through my hearing aid, I could make out a faint sound, something I had never experienced before: *pop-pop-pop*. The *pops* were gunshots. We raced into the clubhouse, where we were put on lockdown. There were three other Americans on the team: Kimera Bartee, Jim Dedrick, and bench coach Dave Jauss. After we had been told that yes, gunshots had been fired, we were all freaking out.

When we eventually came out of the clubhouse and looked around, we saw a chaotic scene. The field was messed up and it looked like a riot had broken out. It was frightening. I desperately wanted the at bats the Venezuelan League would provide, and believed it was best for my career, but at that moment, for the first time, I began to wonder if there was more to life than being a Major League Baseball player.

It was the spring after playing winter ball in Venezuela that I ended up signing with the Tigers and made their major-league team out of Spring Training, so maybe the additional winter reps paid dividends. But I had to wonder if it was worth risking my life. Even as harrowing as Venezuela was, I loved experiencing a different culture in a faraway place.

I also had one other experience playing baseball internationally. After rehabbing from the surgery on my wrist in 1999, I went to Mexico that winter to play for the Navojoa Mayos in the Mexican Winter League. Navojoa is a city of about 160,000 people, located in the Sonora region of Mexico, about five hundred miles south of Phoenix. Playing in Navojoa was a terrific experience. From the housing accommodations to the stadium, to the local food and street vendors, everything about it was fun and interesting. Our team ended up winning the championship, and the entire city celebrated with us. It was estimated that there were about one hundred thousand people at the victory celebration.

CHAPTER 17

Starting Over in Montreal . . . and Beyond

After I finished the 2000 season in Albuquerque strongly, Joe obtained a couple of offers for me for the 2001 season and I decided to rejoin the Montreal Expos organization, where I had gotten my memorable first major-league hit eight years earlier. I figured I would probably start the season in Triple-A Ottawa, but if I did well, a call-up to Montreal would likely soon follow. Sure enough, I hit .333 in my first twenty-two games in Ottawa and was called up to Montreal in early May.

Felipe Alou was still the manager of the Expos, and I immediately felt comfortable as he welcomed me back to the team, assuring me I would be getting plenty of playing time. True to his word, Felipe started me in almost every game in May, and in most of them, he had me batting leadoff or second in the batting order. I flourished the entire month. I got three hits off future Hall of Famer Greg Maddux on May 30 to raise my average to .327.

My confidence was soaring, and I fully expected this go-round in Montreal to be a very successful season for me. What changed everything is that the same night after my three-hit game versus Maddux, Expos owner Jeffrey Loria fired Felipe Alou. When news reached the clubhouse that he had been let go, there was a feeling of shock and

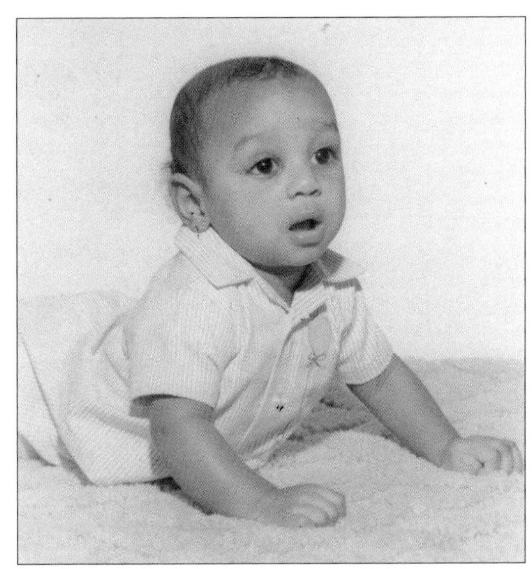

An early baby photo of me at approximately five months old.
(Photo Credit: Family Photo)

preschool playing with friend Alisa Fleetwood.
hoto Credit: William Mills)

Getting ready to hit a fastball at age eight!
(Photo Credit: Sallie Pride)

The Wheaton Boys Club 1975 "Sluggers" baseball team. Don Stein—the terrific coach who taught me so much about baseball—is in the top row with the baseball cap. *(Photo Credit: Don Stein)*

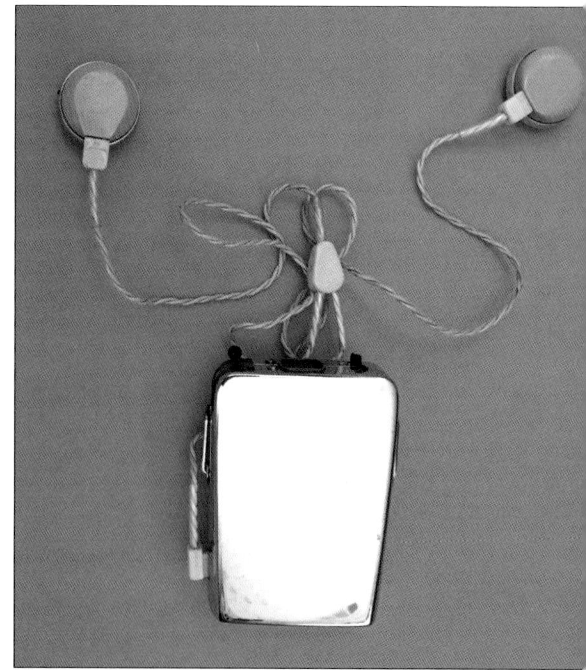

The clunky, cumbersome hearing aid I wore in a pouch strapped to my chest while playing T-Ball and Little League baseball. *(Photo Credit: Sallie Pride)*

Driving in for a layup during a Kennedy High School basketball game.
(Photo Credit: Courtesy of John F. Kennedy High School)

With many of the athletic trophies and awards I received during my childhood and teenage years.
(Photo Credit: Sallie Pride)

At dinner with New York Mets scout Carmen Fusco after signing my first professional baseball contract with the Mets.
(Photo Credit: Courtesy of Carmen Fusco)

The historic letter issued by t
New York Mets allowing r
to attend college and also pl
professional baseball duri
my college summer breal
*(Photo Credit: John Pri
and the New York Me*

NEW YORK NATIONAL LEAGUE BASEBALL CLUB

OPERATED BY DOUBLEDAY SPORTS, INC.

SHEA STADIUM, NEW YORK, NY 11368

BUSINESS OFFICE — (718) 507-METS • TICKET OFFICE — (718) 507-TIXX • TWX: 710-582-2496

ROLAND JOHNSON
DIRECTOR OF SCOUTING

June 23, 1986

Mr. John Pride
1709 Woodwell Road
Silver Springs, MD 20906

Dear Mr. Pride:

It was very gratifying to me to recently sign your son, Curtis, to a professional baseball contract with the New York Mets.

We, the New York Mets, hereby give permission to Curtis to participate in intercollegiate basketball at the College of William and Mary and will not interfere in any way during his academic school year and basketball season.

He will be expected to play in our organization from May 15 to August 15 of each year until graduation from William and Mary. He will then be expected to play on a full time basis. However, as we discussed in earlier conversations, please keep an open mind as to a longer period of participation each year with the Mets as Curtis begins to make progress in baseball.

Curtis has the tools to be a Major League player and we all look forward to working with him.

Regards,

Roland Johnson

Roland Johnson
Director of Scouting

RJ/ mjh

cc: J. Barr
C. Fusco
J. McIlvaine
S. Schryver

Driving to the basket and scoring for the William & Mary basketball team.
(Photo Credit: Courtesy of Villiam & Mary Athletic Department)

duation day at William & Mary.
oto Credit: Sallie Pride)

With Dad and Mom and sisters Christine and Jacqui.
(Photo Credit: Family Photo)

With my Mom and Dad and legendary astronaut and U.S. Senator John Glenn and his wife Annie.
(Photo Credit: John Pride)

My terrific parents, John and Sallie Pride. *(Photo Credit: Family Photo)*

tealing second base for the Harrisburg Senators. *(Photo Credit: Courtesy of Senators Partners, LLC)*

With my lifelong best frie
Steve Gru
(Photo Credit: Steve Gru

Tipping my batting helmet in acknowledgment of the lengthy standing ovation from the sold-out crowd in Montreal's Olympic Stadium after my first major league hit.
(Photo Credit: Courtesy of Curtis Pride

With my awesome long-time agent and advisor, Joe Strasser. *(Photo Credit: Sallie Pride)*

Signing autographs before a game. *(Photo Credit: Sallie Pride)*

Narrowly beating a pick-off throw to first base while playing for the Detroit Tigers.
(Photo Credit: Ted Mathias/ AFP via Getty Images)

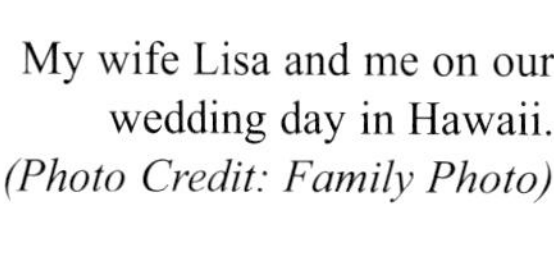

My wife Lisa and me on our wedding day in Hawaii.
(Photo Credit: Family Photo)

Starting my swing at an incoming pitch while playing for the Atlanta Braves.
(Photo Credit: Al Bello/Allsport/Getty Images)

A running over-the-shoulder catch deep in the gap near the outfield wall in Yankee Stadium.
(Photo Credit: Ezra Shaw/Getty Images)

Knocking in a walk-off game winning RBI for the New York Yankees to beat the Boston Red Sox.
(Photo Credit: Ezra Shaw/Getty Images)

With Michael Jordan, who invited me to play in numerous impromptu pick-up basketball games during our several months playing in the Arizona Fall Baseball League.
(Photo Credit: Lisa Pride)

ıg doused with champagne celebrating an American ıc West Division pionship with my ngeles Angels teammates. *o Credit: Brad Mangin/ Photos via Getty Images)*

king with my daughter Noelle after a game for the Angels. *(Photo Credit: Lisa Pride)*

With President Barack Obama, First Lady Michelle Obama,
Vice President Joe Biden, and Michelle Kwan in the White House.
(Photo Credit: Courtesy of the White House Photo Office)

With the greatest of all-time, Muhammad Ali. *(Photo Credit: Diego Lopez)*

Coaching the Gallaudet University baseball team. *(Photo Credit: Courtesy of Gallaudet University Athletics/ David Sinclair)*

Me happy as can be fly fishing. *(Photo Credit: John Pride)*

With my terrific family, Lisa, Noelle, and Colten. *(Photo Credit: Pride family photo)*

With David Van Sleet, President and General Manager of the Louisville Slugger Warriors baseball team, after winning the Las Vegas Open MSBL Championship. The Warriors are a team of players with disabilities (mostly amputees) that I have had the honor of coaching for the past several years. *(Photo Credit: David Van Sleet)*

A celebration at home plate with teammates Jamie Foxx, J.K. Simmons, Terry Crews and others after hitting a home run in the MLB All-Star Legends and Celebrity Softball Game. *(Photo Credit (Mark Cunningham/ MLB Photos via Getty Images)*

disappointment. We all liked Felipe. He was a wonderful guy and a great manager, and as players we felt like we had let him down.

We were doubly shocked when we heard that Jeff Torborg had been hired as his replacement. Torborg had been working as an analyst for Fox TV and had been handpicked by Loria. When a manager is brought in from outside the organization, it usually means changes are in store. True to form, Torborg shook things up and decided to give another outfielder on the team, Mark Smith, most of my playing time.

Even though I had raised my batting average to an even higher .333 with another good game as the starting left fielder in Torborg's first game as manager, he began to use me primarily as a pinch hitter, which is an extremely tough role. I started only four times in Torborg's first twenty games as manager, and two of those were as the designated hitter against an American League team. As the summer progressed, I began to feel my career slipping away, the clock ticking, my skills atrophying. Frustrated, I asked for a meeting with Torborg to clear the air and find out what I could do to get back in the organization's good graces.

The Expos general manager, Jim Beattie, also came to the meeting in Torborg's office, and their response was to tell me they were designating me for an assignment back to Triple-A Ottawa. There was one problem, though. Since it was early September, the minor-league season was already over. So, basically, the Expos were sending me home. I had been released, even if I'd been spared the humiliation of having that word said to my face. To this day, what happened that season in Montreal after Jeff Torborg replaced Felipe Alou remains the most surprising and mysterious thing that happened to me during my entire career in professional baseball.

What then made that timeframe even more chaotic and memorable is after the Expos sent me packing, Lisa and I decided to stop at Niagara Falls for a few days' vacation on our long drive from Montreal back home to Florida. We were at Niagara Falls on September 11, 2001, the day of the terrorist attacks on the United States. Being directly on the border between the United States and Canada, we had to stay at Niagara Falls several days longer than we had planned as we watched all the news unfold. It made that horrific day in our nation's history even more unforgettable for Lisa and me.

After the depressing end to my 2001 season in Montreal and the attacks of 9/11, I was on the free agent market again in 2002. At that time Brian Graham was the senior director of player development for the Pittsburgh Pirates, and I had gotten to know him during his previous work as a minor-league manager in the Cleveland Indians organization. We always liked and had a mutual respect for each other, so Brian offered me a contract to play for the Pirates Triple-A team in Nashville, Tennessee.

Since the Pirates were going to be in a rebuilding mode with younger players at the major-league level, I knew that my time in Nashville would likely not result in a call-up to Pittsburgh that season. Nevertheless, I saw it as an opportunity to get my career back on track after the bad taste that was still in my mouth from Montreal.

After playing at least a part of six of the previous seven years in the majors (only missing 1999 due to injury), I still anticipated that the season in Nashville was going to be a big adjustment. You never want to go back to Triple-A: The travel is harder. You fly to most of the away games, but it's commercial, with a lot of early-morning flights, the kind where you wake up at 4:00 a.m. and board a plane ninety minutes later.

You would play a night game, unwind, then hit the sack for a couple of hours before the alarm rang. Then it was off to the airport for the first flight of the day. You would get to the next town, check in to an average to second-rate hotel, and head straight to the ballpark. Don't get me wrong, it beats many other types of work, and I wouldn't trade those years for anything, but your sleep cycle is never quite right.

In the minor leagues your quality of life goes down in every respect. The worst part is the mental anguish, especially as an older player. You worry that you will begin to be perceived as a has-been, someone whose time has come and gone. Throughout my career I was spared the indignity of officially being released, but I always knew the score. My first experience with rejection came when I left the Mets. I chose to leave the organization as a six-year free agent, but, really, it was not my decision. I left because the Mets had no plans for me, and I knew it.

I also knew that the Pirates, who once had their eye on drafting me, now had no long-term plans for me, either. But I still went to Nashville in the right frame of mind and had a good season, hitting .296 in 110 games, with ten home runs, plus twenty-two stolen bases. After the 2002 season in Nashville ended, I was now a thirty-three-year-old minor-league free agent, which is significantly past the average age for signing a Triple-A contract. During that winter's offseason Joe was pretty much told by every major-league organization: "Sorry, but we want to go in a younger direction in Triple-A this year."

So that spring I swallowed my pride and signed with the Nashua Pride of the independent Atlantic League. I had enjoyed my previous short time in Nashua when I was coming back from my wrist surgery in 1999 and was hoping against hope that I could catch the eye of a big-league team once more.

It was another setback, but nothing I hadn't experienced before. My playing career was filled with calls to the manager's office where I was told there was no room for me on the big-league roster and I would be going to the minors. It was always hard, even after you had heard the standard spiel over and over. It was always the same thing, more or less.

"You are not getting a lot of playing time and we think it is impeding your development," a manager would say. "We want you to get more at bats, get your confidence up. Be ready. We want you back up here with the big club."

When you're young, it all sounds great. Then, after you've heard the same song-and-dance routine a few times, it all just seems like a broken record. Invariably, you walk out of the manager's office deflated. It's up to you to rebound, to get your head right, start all over and find a way back to the big leagues. Many players go to independent ball with a sense of resignation, as they already know it's the end of the line. My outlook saved me. I saw going to an independent team as a good opportunity to prove I could still play and intended to make the most of it.

I also fell in love with the city of Nashua, New Hampshire. Located about an hour from Boston, Nashua was a charming, clean, safe place, and Holman Stadium was a nice ballpark. Nashua had been voted one of the best places to live in America, and it was easy to see why.

Butch Hobson was the manager at Nashua, and he treated me very well. I also knew some guys from playing minor-league ball. Chris English, the owner, had other businesses, a financial corporation in New York, and he traveled back and forth. If things didn't work out, I figured it would be a good place to end my career. You reach a point in your career when looking for a team is like looking for a cemetery plot. Nashua, I thought, would be a good place for my baseball career to die.

Once I got there, of course, I played like my very life depended on it. I did that every time I was let go—the only real reason I can find to explain why my career lasted twenty-three seasons. The greatest, most unlikely, Houdini act of my career was about to unfold. I got off to a torrid start at Nashua, tearing up independent-league pitching to the tune of a .344 batting average in my first sixteen games. The New York Yankees liked what they saw and signed me to a contract with their Triple-A affiliate in Columbus, Ohio.

I got off to a fast start in Columbus, and soon thereafter my phone vibrated, and another dream came true: The Yankees were summoning me to the Bronx.

CHAPTER 18

Pride of the Yankees

On a hot, muggy morning in July 2003, I walked out the front door of the Roger Smith Hotel into the dizzying hustle of Midtown Manhattan. While I could not experience the sounds of the big city—cabs whizzing along Lexington Avenue, car horns honking, tourists and locals chatting as they made their way along the sidewalks—I could feel them. I had been here before, as a member of the visiting team, and the feeling was always the same. The expressions on the faces of pedestrians, the putrid exhaust of busses, the pace of the traffic, and the inviting aroma of street food wafting from the carts of vendors, all told me this was a place that moved at its own speed, a place where I needed to keep my senses on high alert.

My guard up, I made a beeline to the nearest newsstand, where I grabbed a copy of the *New York Post*, handed the attendant a dollar, and flipped through the pages, looking for the sports section. I have always been a news junkie and love keeping up with what's going on in the world. Honestly, though, I wanted to see if my recall had made the papers, almost as if I needed validation that I was really a New York Yankee. I still wasn't sure this was really happening.

Finally I found it on the back page, a headline too good to be true, one that felt it had been made up on a home computer: CURTIS TO BE LATEST PRIDE OF THE YANKEES.

That was good. That was the *New York Post.* I had always loved the movie *The Pride of the Yankees,* with Gary Cooper, and seeing my name associated with an iconic baseball franchise and a classic movie, all in one clever headline, sent chills up my spine.

After reading newspapers in countless minor- and major-league cities while dealing with reporters around batting cages and in clubhouses, I knew a little bit about how the media worked. Mine was an inspirational, feel-good story, the kind that was catnip to sportswriters and their editors. As long as I continued to play the game "the right way," with hustle and heart, they would continue to be in my corner. But this was the *New York Post,* the most shameless of tabloids. I knew one little slip, one stupid error, would probably lead to an equally clever headline that highlighted my misdeeds. And my "feel good" story might not feel so good to the New York sportswriters.

I had come to accept my deafness as equal-parts blessing and burden. Yes, it enabled me to tune out negative voices and made my remaining senses sharper, but that meant seeing something in print resonated deeper, thundering through my body, rocking my world like an earthquake. I didn't want anything to rattle the redemption I was feeling.

I was thirty-four years old, had appeared in 349 big-league games for four different teams over seven seasons, but walking along the streets of Midtown Manhattan as a Yankee made me feel like my baseball career had been born again. New York had always been the place where dreams come true, where aspiring artists and musicians gravitated to hone their craft, where actors made a name in the theater, where executives in banking and media reached the pinnacle of their industry. I believed the same held true for an athlete, particularly for a baseball player. To me, Yankee Stadium was Times Square, Broadway, and Wall Street, all rolled into one.

So far in my career, I had played for the Red Sox, in one of the great baseball cities of the world; for the Tigers, in a city with a rich baseball history; and for the Braves, a team that was a regional favorite throughout the South, with games televised nationally on one of the world's first superstations. None of that, however, compared to the rush of New York City, of donning the sport's most iconic uniform and playing in its most historic ballpark.

Appearing in the famous pinstripes was beyond anything I had envisioned, something too impossible to even contemplate. But this was real and seeing the *New York Post* story was just the start of my time in a fantasy world. There was a part of me that felt a sense of vindication. When the New York Mets drafted me out of Kennedy High School, I had dreams of a grand career, in the grandest city in the world. When it didn't happen, when the Mets cut me loose while I was still in their minor-league system, it felt like a dream interrupted, one that could never be fulfilled.

But here I was, in Midtown, staying in the same hotel the Yankees had used to house legendary players when they first joined the club. Less than twenty-four hours earlier in Columbus, I had been held out of the lineup. The Yankees had decided to send pitcher Brandon Claussen to Triple-A to keep him sharp and I was selected to replace him on their big-league roster, largely because I was considered a reliable, experienced outfielder.

There was one catch. As soon as Nick Johnson came off the disabled list, I would be sent back to Columbus. But because of the length of my previous big-league experience, I could reject going back to Triple-A and instead opt for free agency. The Yankees did not want that to happen, so they wanted assurance from me that I would waive my right to become a free agent.

I had begun the 2003 season at Nashua, with no guarantee I would ever see my name on a big-league roster again. It was my second stint at Nashua, a baseball purgatory most players never break away from. While I had a soft spot in my heart for Nashua, that was tempered by the possibility it represented the end of the road. Just three months earlier, I was dogged by the fear I would go to a lower minor-league team and play down to the level of competition, soon finding myself lost in the oblivion of the independent leagues.

But I bet on myself, and after hitting .344 with five home runs and twenty-five RBIs in just sixteen games at Nashua, I caught the eye of the Yankees. My faith in the universe, and my place in it, had been restored.

I was back in the game, even if I wasn't really all the way in. After starting the season in the baseball backwaters, I wasn't about to turn down a chance to play on the game's biggest stage, even if it was just for a cameo appearance, so I agreed to the condition that I would go back to Triple-A. Besides, I had something inside that the Yankees could not take away: the belief that I could still play big-league ball, faith that things would work out. The Yankees planned on me going back to Columbus by week's end. I believed otherwise.

I took the subway to old Yankee Stadium, the train clattering down the tracks, beneath the streets of the Upper East Side, ducking in and out of darkness, before pulling up to the 161st Street Yankee Stadium Subway Station. The car was crowded and sultry, people jammed shoulder to shoulder, and I swear, to me, it was better than any ride at Disneyland.

The short walk from the elevated station to the ballpark was surreal, the stadium and my destiny looming larger with each step. Babe Ruth had made that walk, Lou Gehrig and Reggie Jackson, too. I was only supposed to fill out the roster, maybe enter a game as a late-inning defensive replacement, but I still had my dreams. I believed this could be the break I had waited for the previous two years when I hadn't been able to get another taste of the big leagues.

Yankee Stadium was gorgeous and historic and everything the soul of the game ought to be. I had played there before as a member of visiting teams, but on this day it took on an entirely new aura, like the difference between looking at a model of your dream house and moving into it. This felt like home.

After checking in with the security guard, I took the narrow staircase down two levels, to the basement, walked down a hallway and entered the clubhouse. There they were, pin-striped uniforms hanging in every locker.

I poked my head in manager Joe Torre's office. Torre had become synonymous with the Yankees' recent success, a steadying hand in often-turbulent waters. I was never the type to be starstruck, but Torre possessed all the characteristics I admired, and I desperately wanted him to live up to his image. This was a man devoid of ego, despite a great playing career; a guy who understood the game as well as anyone; someone who always displayed great equanimity—both in the dugout and in his dealings with the media.

Torre lived up to my starry-eyed expectations of him. "Congratulations, Curtis, and welcome to the Yankees," he said. "We think you can help us win. Stay ready."

Then he gave me a rundown of the rules. Hair to be neatly trimmed at all times. No facial hair. The dress code included wearing a coat and tie on all travel days.

"Yes, sir," I said.

Torre could have told me to come to the ballpark in my uniform and then wash it in my hotel room's sink, and I would have gladly done it.

I went back to my locker, where Derek Jeter quickly stopped by.

"Welcome to New York," the captain said. Derek and I had lived in the same Mesa, Arizona, condo complex during the Arizona Fall League, where we had become friendly. He greeted me with the warmth of an old friend, but with the fire of a leader I wanted to follow.

Derek was the captain of the Yankees, but he didn't need to have a C on his jersey. It was obvious he was a leader by the way he carried himself. You could tell by the way teammates responded when he said something. Derek had game, of course, but he had much more than that. He was smart and seemed to have an answer for everything: how to handle the media, how to deal with fans away from the ballpark, what to do with your money, how to stay in shape in the offseason.

It wasn't just that Derek had all the answers, it was that he was the walking, talking example of how to be a Yankee. Even though Derek seemed to make all the right moves, he never came off as a know-it-all, never displayed any arrogance. He remains one of my favorite people in the game, and anytime I think back on any of the taunting and abuse I took along the way, I think about how well Derek Jeter treated everyone, and how the people who are the most secure and confident in themselves don't have a need to haze or abuse others.

Bernie Williams stopped by and so did David "Boomer" Wells. I knew Bernie was an all-time good guy, but I was surprised to look up from my locker to see David asking if I needed anything. David had a reputation for being a bit flakey, for being one of the great characters of the game, and I thought maybe it was an act he cultivated for attention. But Boomer turned out to be a wonderful teammate, the kind of guy you'd go the extra mile for when he was on the mound.

After being welcomed by some modern-day Yankee legends, there was only one thing left to do: go pay my respects to the Yankee legends of yesterday. I walked across the lush outfield grass to Monument Park, where plaques and retired numbers honored the team's all-time greats. The monuments were originally situated in the field of play, before being moved behind the outfield fence during the 1970s renovation of the stadium. Now the names and numbers served as a de facto, open-air Hall of Fame: Mickey Mantle, Joe DiMaggio, Yogi Berra, Whitey Ford. And on, and on, and on.

A midseason call-up for a quick jolt of espresso wouldn't get me a plaque in Monument Park, but if I could get into a game, it would get me a small place in the Yankees history and family. When I returned to the clubhouse, I saw my name someplace that seemed monumental to me: on the lineup card. There it was, in black Sharpie, batting eighth in that day's game: **PRIDE, R.F.**

It was the Fourth of July holiday weekend, a picture-perfect, warm, blue-sky Sunday afternoon. Not only that, but we were also playing the Yankees' longtime archrival, the Boston Red Sox. There was a palpable energy in the sold-out stadium, even before the game began. Like all teams, the Yankees kept detailed scouting reports and statistical information on all the pitchers in the league. John Burkett had been announced as the Red Sox starter that day, so before the game I carefully studied his various pitches and tendencies.

In my first at bat, I worked the count to 3–2 and then hit a line drive into the gap in left center field, where Manny Ramirez made an excellent over-the-shoulder running catch, robbing me of a certain double or triple. In my next at bat, I hit a sharp ground out to the first baseman. I was seeing Burkett's pitches well and felt totally locked into the game.

My next at bat was as the leadoff hitter in the bottom of the sixth inning. Both starting pitchers were pitching well—Burkett for the Red Sox and Andy Pettitte for us— and we were holding on to a slim 3–1 lead. Burkett threw me a high slider on the first pitch, which I fouled back to the screen. On the next pitch he threw me a tantalizing, extremely slow curveball, which I took outside for ball one.

Often, after a pitcher throws a slow curveball, he assumes the hitter will be looking for a fastball on the next pitch. So, in the never-ending cat-and-mouse game between pitcher and batter, he will sometimes follow up with another slow pitch, often a changeup, hoping the hitter will be fooled into thinking it is a fastball and swing too early, either missing the pitch entirely, or be off balance and hit a weak ground out or pop-up. But, as I had seen in my pregame study of the scouting report, Burkett liked to throw his changeup early in the count, so I mentally prepared myself for that possibility, thinking, *Be patient. Wait for it to arrive in the strike zone.*

Sure enough, as the next pitch left Burkett's hand, I read the rotation immediately as a changeup, and patiently kept my weight back and firmly balanced as I swung. I timed it perfectly. The ball jumped off my bat, high into the air, to the deepest part of Yankee Stadium, in dead center field. I thought I had gotten it all, but it was 408 feet to the Yankee Stadium center-field wall, so as I sprinted to first base, I kept my eyes on Red Sox center fielder Johnny Damon as he tracked the ball and kept drifting back toward the wall. Finally he was at the wall and jumped, but the ball was well past his reach. As I was nearing second base, I saw it bounce at least twenty feet into the air off the hard ground over the wall, near the legendary monuments.

I couldn't hear the fifty-five thousand fans cheering for me as I rounded the bases, but as in Montreal, when I got my first major-league hit, I could feel them. Alfonso Soriano, the on-deck batter, gave me a big high five as I reached home plate, and Derek Jeter was also waiting for me outside the dugout with a fist-bump high five. Then after I went down the line of high fives from my teammates in the dugout, I looked for a seat, but Ruben Sierra motioned to me that the fans were standing and continuing to cheer and wanted me to come out for a curtain call. David Wells then sealed the deal by gently pushing me up the dugout steps.

I bounded up the three steps, barely touching them, then stood outside the dugout for a moment, where I doffed my helmet and held it up to the fans. In the thousands of faces before me, I could see how much the Yankees meant to them. I also saw something else: warmth, affection, pure joy. Fifty-five thousand fans thrilled that a member of their favorite team had just homered, excited that the unlikeliest of long shots had just come in. Those Yankee fans, people from all over the tristate area, from working-class Staten Island to the wealthy Upper East Side, from the hardscrabble Jersey Shore to the tony Hamptons, were giving me my moment.

And in that moment I realized the moment wasn't mine at all. It was ours.

After the game I spoke with a cluster of reporters gathered around my locker, who all wanted to interview me. Then I rode the elevator up to ground level and met my family outside the stadium. Lisa was up from Florida, my parents made the trip from Silver

Spring, and my sister Christine, who lives and works in New York, was there also.

I made the same two-block walk to the 161st Street Yankee Stadium Subway Station, this time with an entourage of family and through a gauntlet of well-wishers. I entered the Bronx an unknown, and now I was departing with a small piece of Yankee lore to call my own.

Fans reached out to touch me, as if I were the pope, and interacting with me might offer a miracle of their own. I could read their lips. "Way to go!" some said. "Great game!" was on the lips of others. It was all too much.

We hopped on the subway, back into Manhattan—my family and I and a train car full of raucous, rowdy Yankee fans—them believing they were sharing my moment with me, and me knowing I was lucky enough to share a small moment in their world with them.

As the train rolled into Midtown, my father hit me with a newly minted trivia question: "Who is the only player to hit a home run in his first game for the Boston Red Sox in Fenway Park and his first game for the New York Yankees in Yankee Stadium?" Then he gave the answer: "My son!"

Back in Manhattan, my family and I stepped off the train, onto the platform to one last ovation from the subway faithful, then headed off to a late-night celebration of our own. At Blue Smoke Barbecue, we ordered platters of ribs with all the fixings, passed it around family style, pairing it with cold beer to create a memory that warms me still. A night without limits in the city that never sleeps; baseball, deafness, and good food bringing a family together for a celebration that never would have happened without a whole lot of faith—my family's in me, which led to mine in myself, creating a belief so strong, the mighty New York Yankees became a part of it, too.

The next morning I rose with the sun at the Roger Smith Hotel, thinking it was possibly still all a dream. I walked through the lobby, stepped out onto Lexington Avenue, and made my way to that same corner newsstand. There I grabbed the *New York Post,* flipped to the back page, again looking for confirmation that it had really happened.

It had.

There it was, as big and bold as the city itself, a full-color photograph of me tipping my hat to the crowd. The image totally covered the newspaper's entire back page, with the *New York Post*'s headline saying it better than I could, all in four very large, simple, spine-tingling words: PRIDE OF THE YANKEES!

CHAPTER 19

Playing for Pride

It was December 2003 and the excitement of the home run for the Yankees a few months before had worn off. I had gone back to Columbus, as agreed, and done well, finishing the season with a .289 batting average in fifty-five games. But I was turning thirty-five, and for the first time, I began to sense the years of my baseball career becoming mileage on my own personal odometer. No longer was I learning, gaining experience, and getting better. Instead, my natural athletic gifts were beginning to decline. Speed had always given me an edge in every aspect of the game, but now it was waning. So, too, was my bat speed, which meant if I were to get back to the big leagues, it would be with a combination of using my mind and experience, along with my body.

Lisa made me a cake and took me out to dinner for my birthday on December 17, but I couldn't find any reason to celebrate. My mind wandered all night long. At an age when most people were hitting their stride professionally, like many athletes, I was coming to terms with the fact that my career had peaked. I was terrified that my playing days might be over, uncertain of what a future without baseball might hold. The game had become such a vital part of my identity—while others saw a deaf man, I saw a good defensive outfielder with excellent speed and a quick bat. Here I was, out on a special occasion with my terrific wife, and all I could do was think about the possible passing of a baseball career that was on life support.

At that point in my life, I lacked perspective, so instead of enjoying the evening celebrating a milestone with my wife, I was sullen and aloof, wondering if I'd have a team to play for when Spring Training opened. Baseball was my identity, and without it I feared I was just another deaf guy.

The entire offseason played out in a similar fashion. Joe Strasser was regularly calling teams, and every time my phone vibrated, I was hoping it was him texting to tell me about a new opportunity. But the holidays came and went without an invitation, and when Joe summarized everything for me in late March, it looked like my only option was going to be a return to Nashua.

I had been through this before, falling so far and hard that the only landing spot was a team in the independent league. Once before I had clawed my way out of baseball's dungeon, back to the major leagues, my game too impressive to be ignored. But no one, to my knowledge, had ever gone to an independent team three times and made it back to the big leagues twice. Could I rally again to accomplish something that had never been done before?

For the first time I felt closer to the end than the beginning and wondered if it was time to walk away on my own terms. After I talked to Lisa, I decided to bet on myself and play one more year with Nashua. My game would be the ultimate decider; if I proved to be good enough, someone would find me, just like they always had. If not, I could get on with my life, knowing I'd given the game my physical prime, and now, with my college degree, I could comfortably move on to a new career.

I had heard a lot of stories about players putting up big numbers for an independent-league team and getting called up—heck, I had done it once before—so that's what I tried to focus my attention on. Still, in my gut I couldn't deny I was starting to doubt I would ever get back to the big leagues.

I was back at Holman Stadium in Nashua, which was every bit as charming as I remembered. Nestled in a picturesque, wooded area, it struck me as being like something out of a Norman Rockwell painting. In a way I felt like I was going back to a time and place when I knew I still had the tools to get back to the big leagues.

If you were to paint a picture of baseball as America's national pastime, you could do worse than using Holman Stadium as your model. Yet, for all the glorious splendor that surrounded the stadium, the clubhouse was its own world, populated by dreamers with no shot at ever making it to the big leagues.

There was something almost mystical about playing for Nashua. The team there was known as the Pride, which meant I could play for both the name on the front of my jersey and the one on the back at the same time. It may sound corny, but I've always felt honored to carry the name Pride on the back of my jersey. I liked it mostly because I was representing my family, but also because I felt like the name—and everyone it stood for—challenged me to be a walking definition of the very word.

I am a man of faith, and pride is one of the seven deadly sins, but I never really cared for that definition. I prefer Webster's first entry for "pride": *the quality or state of being proud*. That was me. I was nothing if not proud—proud of my name, my family, and the circumstances I had to overcome. Now, however, with my big-league future in doubt, I was having trouble living up to the name that was my birthright.

Yet, when I arrived in Florida for Spring Training with the rest of the Nashua team, I had to stave off the temptation to submit to the part of my name that was a sin. I had played in the big leagues and believed that's where I belonged, so I reported with a chip on my shoulder—one big enough to make me, sometimes, look like a prideful jerk. My goal was to get out of Nashua and back to the big leagues as soon as possible, but my teammates, coaches, and management were so supportive, I couldn't help but fall in love with my role in Nashua. It was such a magical setting and the folks there were so supportive, I began to wonder if I had found my destiny.

Young teammates, who knew I had played in the big leagues, came to me for advice, and I began to embrace the role of elder statesman and mentor. Most of my teammates were surviving on a dream and little else. They arrived with the same high hopes I had. While their chances of playing at a higher level were long, they wanted to give it everything they had, and I enjoyed helping them. I came to like my role so much that I no longer felt any pressure to get back to The Show and began to feel at peace with my place in the baseball world. Then a funny thing happened: I began to tear the cover off the ball. When my parents drove up to New Jersey from Silver Spring to see a game, my father marveled that the scoreboard showed my batting average to be 1.000. Through the first three games, I had reached base eleven straight times, with seven hits and four walks.

In my first seventeen games with the Pride, I hit .446, with a .513 OBP and .613 slugging percentage, for an OPS of 1.144. Then The Call came once again. This time it was the Anaheim Angels reaching out to me. Bill Stoneman, their general manager, had been assistant general manager for the Expos when I made my big-league debut and we had maintained a good relationship. The Angels told me they had been monitoring my play in Nashua, had always liked my professionalism and reliability, and wanted to sign me to a minor-league deal.

It had been eleven years since I first received The Call to join the Expos for my big-league debut, but this call was every bit as sweet, maybe even sweeter. Making that day even more special, in an incredible coincidence Lisa had flown up to Nashua that same morning and was able to tell me personally, before I left for Salt Lake City, the great news that she was pregnant with our first child.

After I signed the contract, the Angels assigned me to Triple-A Salt Lake City, and told me that if I performed well, they wouldn't hesitate to bring me to Anaheim. The Salt Lake Bees would be the twenty-fourth team I had played for, and I didn't want them to be the last, so I treated it like my career was beginning, not ending. I was one of the first players to arrive at the ballpark every day, took early batting practice, and hit the weight room hard.

Because I had spent so much time preparing, once the games started, I was completely relaxed and swung the bat as well as I ever had. It didn't take long for the Angels to notice. In nineteen games at Salt Lake, I hit .431, with an OPS again over 1.000 at 1.142. In June, Stoneman sent word to Salt Lake that I was wanted in Anaheim.

The Angels were in the middle of a pennant race, and they thought I could help. Back in 1993, the Expos gambled on me, believing my game would translate to the major leagues, and I will be forever appreciative. The Angels, however, weren't gambling: They looked at my track record and placed a bet that I could help them win. They knew I would work hard, be good in the clubhouse, play good defense, and provide the occasional offensive spark. That endorsement felt good. I felt like me again.

When I arrived at Angel Stadium, manager Mike Scioscia called me into his office. "Be ready," he said. "We brought you up because there is a role for you on this team. I won't hesitate to call on you in any situation."

Scioscia wasn't lying. The Angels were battling the Oakland Athletics, or A's, for first place in the American League West, and as the season wound down, each game felt like a playoff game. We traveled to Texas in late September, tied with the A's.

In the third game of that crucial series with the Rangers, I had entered the game in the middle innings as a replacement for center fielder Garret Anderson, who had gotten hurt. That's when I stepped to the plate for one of the biggest at bats of my career. The date was September 29, 2004; there were two outs in the ninth inning, and we were trailing the Rangers, 6–5. Vladimir Guerrero had gotten a hit, so we had the tying run on first base. But the Rangers had their All-Star closer Francisco Cordero on the mound, which usually meant the game was all but over.

Cordero's first pitch was a slider, low and inside. As I stepped back into the batter's box, I began telling myself, *Get a pitch you can hit. Stay focused. You have done this before; you can do it again!*

The next pitch from Cordero was a fastball, low and at the knees, but right in my wheelhouse. I put a good swing on it, and the ball jumped off my bat on a line to deep center field. It hit the top of the fence on the fly in straightaway center field. The center fielder played the carom well, but since there were two outs, Vladdy was able to run on the crack of the bat and just beat the relay throw home to score the tying run as I sped into third base. As I stood on third base with all my teammates celebrating in the dugout, I realized I had come through in the most difficult of situations: getting a huge hit with two outs in the ninth inning, against one of the major's best closers, to save the game and send it into extra innings.

Troy Glaus later hit a home run in the eleventh inning, and we walked away with an improbable 8–7 win in the season's 158th game. Because we lost the next day in Texas, while the A's won, we would need to take two-out-of-three in Oakland to win the West, which we were able to accomplish. Winning the West with the Angels was a career highlight.

I felt like a big part of that West Division Championship team because that hit was one of many events over the course of the season that enabled the Angels to win the division. If we had lost that game, we would have likely finished the season tied with the A's, forcing a one-game playoff. Instead, we advanced to the postseason.

I think about that at bat from time to time, not because it's one of my greatest glories—which it surely is—but rather to remind myself of the great things that can happen when you maintain faith and keep plugging along. That game-saving hit wasn't so much a testament to my skill as a hitter as it was a monument to my perseverance and dedication. That's how I see it, anyway.

It's one of the reasons I tell kids never give up, never stop believing. Anything is possible if you keep trying.

CHAPTER 20

Travelin' Man

You can tell a lot by looking at the back of someone's baseball card. Just as a fortune teller can read the palm of your hand, a baseball person can tell where a player has been, where he's going, what he's all about, by flipping his card over. Some cards, like Cal Ripken Jr.'s or Derek Jeter's, show stability and stardom. Others show desperation and heartbreak.

When I look at the back of my own baseball card and see all the teams I played for, in cities from New England to Southern California, I see a lot of great memories and a refusal to quit. Playing in an independent league typically serves as a player's final act, but twice I rallied from that level and climbed my way back to the big leagues, a fact almost as unlikely as getting to the majors as a deaf player, to begin with.

Leaving home as a teenager, I had no idea how long and winding my career path would be, how many cities would end up appearing on the back of my baseball card, how many managers and coaches I'd play for, how many players and people I'd cross paths with. I had a different career path in mind, envisioning a steady climb up the ladder of the Mets minor-league system during the summers, while working on my college degree during the winters. I would happily pay my dues in a handful of minor-league cities; then, as a reward Shea Stadium would be my baseball home and New York City would be my permanent address.

As fate would have it, I never played a single game for the Mets, and, but for a brief stay in a Manhattan hotel as a member of the Yankees, I never called New York City home. If you had told me before I left home that June morning in 1986 that I would play twenty-three years and appear in the uniforms of twenty-six different teams, I might not have left home at all. The thought of all that change—all that starting over—would have been too daunting. I probably would have unpacked my bags and chosen to focus on a more stable career in the financial world.

Fortunately, nobody told me what was in store. I hit the road, blissfully unaware of the potholes and detours in my path—and there were many. What I couldn't know is that those obstacles weren't really challenges as much as they were life lessons, and that every delay of the dream steeled my resolve, shaping me into the person I am today.

I'm glad I had no idea how things would work out because I learned something at every stop along the way, experienced different regions of the nation, and became friends with people with whom I had very little in common. It's become one of those clichés I abhor so much to say "the journey is the destination," but in my case it really is true.

Here's a look back at every stop along the way.

Kingsport, Tennessee

The first stop in any player's baseball career stays with them forever, like a first crush. Mine was Kingsport, Tennessee, home of the Appalachian League's Kingsport Mets.

Kingsport is a small town, with a population of around forty thousand. When I was there, the town had a strong odor in the air because of the Eastman Chemical Company. I'm told the odor has been eradicated by stricter environmental laws in recent years, but at the time it was pungent, especially for me because my sense of smell is so strong. Otherwise, it was a beautiful town, in the heart of the picturesque Smoky Mountains. People were very friendly, but that didn't prevent me from becoming homesick.

We traveled by bus, sometimes on trips as long as six hours, and my lasting memory of one of those excursions is of visiting Pulaski, Virginia, home of a minor-league baseball team and apparently more than its share of racists. One day, as I was walking down the street in that city, a car drove by and a guy leaned out the window and I could read his lips yelling "Hey, n-word!" It was the first time I knew of in which that word had been said to me, and I was shocked. I went to a Pizza Hut later that day, walked in the front door, and everyone inside the place stopped what they were doing and stared long and hard at me. There were no words, but their message was clear: You don't belong here. I turned around and walked out, half expecting a knife in my back. Pulaski was a tough town, and from that point on, I just hung around with teammates whenever we went there.

It's funny, when I arrived in Kingsport for my first season, I couldn't wait to be off on my own, out exploring the world, but midway through that first season, I missed my family, and longed for the diversity of Washington, DC. I also missed the privacy of my own room. Everyone on the team lived in a small motel, and my roommate liked to bring local girls back to our room, leaving me with no place to stay. After a few sleepless nights spent on a lawn chair alongside the swimming pool, I decided the $200 I paid in rent entitled me to as much of the room as he. These were things the Mets never warned me about when they came into our living room and sold me on professional baseball.

Later, in my second year, I moved in with a couple named Teresa and Vernon Smith. They had a son who played in the Braves system, and they were a lovely host and hostess for two years. My parents and I then maintained a lifelong friendship with them. In my third and final year in Kingsport, we won the Appalachian League Championship, which made it all worthwhile. And I was named the eighth-best prospect in the Appalachian League by *Baseball America* magazine.

Pittsfield, Massachusetts

My next stop was a short season A-ball team in Pittsfield, Massachusetts, of the New York–Penn League. After my roommate troubles in Kingsport, I was excited to be living with a local family. A woman named Lou Reilly and her daughter, Jeannie, who was four or five years older than I was, had hosted future big leaguers Greg Maddux, Damon Berryhill, and Joe Girardi, and they welcomed me into their home. They both loved the game and instinctively knew when a ballplayer needed support and when he needed space, and it was a great living arrangement. Wahconah Park was a wonderful, historic stadium, where you had to suspend the game for ten minutes every night while the sun set behind the batter's eye. For ten minutes each evening, everyone stopped what they were doing to watch the sunset and appreciate the fact that they were off playing baseball for a (meager) living. It was one of the lowest rungs of baseball—not much glory, not much money—but I was in absolute heaven.

Columbia, South Carolina

A year later, I found myself in Columbia, of the Single-A South Atlantic League. A local resident, Buzz Mathis, was the uncle of a high school friend, Sean Hughes. Buzz and his wife, Flo, offered to take me in as their houseguest. It turned out to be one of the best living experiences of my career. Buzz had a big, beautiful house, just outside town, on Lake Murray, the biggest lake in South Carolina. Buzz had two sons, Michael and Kevin, close to my age, and we would go fishing almost every day. It was a long drive from his house to the ballpark, about an hour, but it was well worth it to live on the lake. The setting was incredibly peaceful, and it was where I realized how calming and therapeutic fishing could be. They had a dock in their backyard, and I absolutely loved being on the water. Before a game, after a game, on the rare off day, you could find me back behind that lake house with a fishing line in the water.

Port St. Lucie, Florida

I wasn't so lucky the next year when I played the entire season in Port St. Lucie, Florida, in the High-A Florida State League. I shared an apartment with three teammates, but the place was big enough that we all had our own rooms, so it worked out okay. While playing in an Instructional League game for the Mets in West Palm Beach against the Atlanta Braves, a funny story occurred that was caused by my deafness.

I was at the plate during a typical midweek game, and the pitcher lost control of a more than ninety-mile-per-hour fastball, which came directly at my head. In that moment instincts take over as you fall backward and your head snaps back to avoid the ball. In this instance, as my head snapped back, the ball lightly glanced off the top of my batting helmet for a hit-by-pitch and automatic awarding of first base. After I jogged down to first and turned around, I saw the umpire motioning to me to come back while rubbing his two palms together in the universally known signal for a "foul ball." Since that play in baseball happens in a matter of milliseconds, you don't have time to drop your bat from the ready-to-hit position, and the umpire thought the ball deflected off the top of my bat, instead of my helmet. So the umpire was motioning that it was a foul ball and directing me to come back to home plate to continue the at bat.

As I was jogging back down the line toward home, I started saying, "No, no. It hit my helmet. It hit my helmet!" But as I arrived face-to-face with the umpire, he started explaining in more detail what he thought he saw. I realized that I couldn't understand what he was saying because he still had his face mask on, and I couldn't read his lips. So I politely told him that I was deaf and asked him to remove his mask so I could read his lips.

He just kept talking, however; so out of frustration I reached out with my right hand and pulled his mask straight out and away from his face so I could read his lips. At the same time I instantaneously remembered the mandatory rule of "never touch an umpire," so I quickly let go of the mask and the strong elastic bands snapped it, hard, right back into his face.

Of course, as would be expected, the umpire instantly gave the dramatic heave-ho signal ("You're outta here!") and threw me out of the game. I started to explain, "No, no, I'm sorry. I didn't do it to hurt or embarrass you. I'm deaf! I'm deaf!" My manager then raced out from the dugout to explain as well. At first, the umpire was skeptical, but when my manager pointed to the hearing aid over my left ear, the umpire calmed down and decided to rescind his ejection and let me back in the game.

However, as I stepped back into the batter's box to continue the at bat, all of us (myself, the pitcher, and the catcher) were continuing to laugh about what had just happened. So I actually wasn't very upset when the umpire called me out on strikes on the next pitch, which was at least five to seven inches outside.

Binghamton, New York

In Binghamton, of the Double-A Eastern League, I initially lived with two other guys and one of their wives, which did not make for the best atmosphere on the home front. Eventually I moved into the home of an older couple, which worked out wonderfully. Phil and Rose Grady were an awesome couple and I never had so much fun with a host family. They had great personalities, were constantly joking around, and had a good time. If not for them, it would have been a miserable season. It was one of my worst seasons on the field, but Phil and Rose made me forget all my problems. I have often been blessed with meeting the nicest people at the right time, and Phil and Rose couldn't have come along at a better time. I would have breakfast and lunch at their house, then head to the ballpark. I would get home late, stopping to pick up food along the way.

Harrisburg, Pennsylvania

Harrisburg was one of my favorite places to play because of the ballpark's location along the Susquehanna River. The fact the park was on an island surrounded by water made for one of my favorite years. For all its beauty and history as Pennsylvania's capital, I will always remember Harrisburg as the place I crossed paths with manager Jim Tracy, one of the best people in or out of baseball. Jim made me feel like his sole purpose in life was to make me a better person and a better player, and I didn't want to betray his investment and confidence in me.

Ottawa, Ontario, Canada

When I played Triple-A ball in Ottawa, I lived with the friend of one of the teachers I worked with at Kennedy High. Diane Anido and her husband, Philip, had three kids and were perfect hosts. They had two boys, Charles and Edward, and one girl, Helene. I became the godfather to Charles. They lived in Rockcliffe, where their neighbors across the street were Dick Pound, who gained fame as an anti-doping expert for the Olympics, and his wife, famous writer Julie Keith. The ballpark was brand-new, and it was really nice. I had a lot of fun in Ottawa, and in my third year there, we won the International League Championship.

Montreal, Quebec, Canada

Montreal will always hold a special place in my heart because it is the city where I made my big-league debut, but even if I never played there, I would still love the place. As it is, Montreal is one of my all-time favorite places to live because the people are nice, the weather in the summer is fantastic, and the fishing is first-rate. The only bad part was Olympic Stadium, which was old and without charm. The Astroturf was worn, and it felt like playing on cement. The best part of playing there was the fishing trips, up by Three Rivers, also known as Trois-Rivières. Bill Stoneman was the vice president/general manager of the team; and, along with coach Jim Tracy and his family and several of the team's media broadcasters, I would join them on fishing trips. We stayed at a cabin a couple of days during the All-Star break and had an absolute blast.

West Palm Beach, Florida

Today I live near West Palm Beach, but I only played three games for the high-level Single-A team there on an injury rehab assignment. In those games I had six hits in eight at bats, so there was no need for me to stay there for further rehab.

My strongest memory of those three games is of Derek Jeter, whom I played against for the first time. It was obvious he was destined for great things. If I could have bought stock in Derek, I would have signed away my entire salary—it was quite obvious that this guy was the total package.

I also will always have fond memories of West Palm Beach, since that is where I first met my wife, Lisa.

Detroit, Michigan

One of the best things about experiencing different cultures is that it allows you to get past broad stereotypes and see the subtle nuances of a place. Detroit has an unfair reputation for being a hard city, but I had a great experience there.

I lived in Dearborn, about twenty minutes from Tiger Stadium. Doug Brocail was a teammate and fellow outdoorsman, and we lived in the same apartment complex. Doug lived with his family, and I lived alone. After every home game we would race back to our apartments and fish in a small pond on-site. Doug was a very good fisherman, and it was always a very spirited competition between the two of us to catch the most bass.

Tiger Stadium was old, and had very small locker rooms, but the impression that stays with me is that unique upper deck that hung over left field. Cecil Fielder was on the team and his young son Prince could hit the ball into the upper deck during batting practice. Guys on the team would make fun of Jody Reed, a five-foot-nine middle infielder, joking that twelve-year-old Prince had more power than he did.

Toledo, Ohio

I only played nine games for the famously named Toledo Mud Hens during a short injury rehab assignment during my 1996 season with the Tigers.

Pawtucket, Rhode Island

Pawtucket was a nice little town, with a charming ballpark that had been completely renovated, and I had a great time there. As with most everyone in the Northeast, people there loved their baseball. Lisa and I rented out the second floor of a house, which was a nice setup. We had our own kitchen and a private area. There was no air-conditioning, and it wasn't very clean, but we were young, had each other, and saw it as a great adventure. When Lisa's father came and installed an air conditioner for us, life got even better.

Boston, Massachusetts

Boston was and is one of the great baseball cities in the world. When I played for the Red Sox, I lived in a hotel close to the ballpark, and loved my walk to Fenway Park, which is a great part of baseball history and a place I had always dreamed about playing in. The Boston fans are incredibly passionate and smart. Fenway Park fans can be demanding, but they were very good to me.

Atlanta, Georgia

When I played for the Braves, Lisa and I rented an apartment in Roswell, just outside of Atlanta. The fly-fishing was great, and Mike Cather, a pitcher on the team, would join me on the Chattahoochee River, one of the longest rivers east of Mississippi, that has some of the best trout fishing in the country. Mike taught me different tricks that helped me become a better fly-fisherman.

Ryan Klesko was on that team, and he and I would go fishing in every city we visited. In Milwaukee, Ryan and I were invited by famous broadcaster Bob Uecker to go fishing with him on his boat.

We took our haul back to the hotel and had the chef at the restaurant cook it. The fish were huge, among the biggest I have ever caught. On the road it was always Ryan and me; when back home in Georgia, it was Mike and me. In Houston, Bobby Cox and Chipper Jones joined Ryan, Mike, and me at a private resort with a twenty-acre pond to fly-fish for bass off a makeshift pontoon boat.

Professional golfer Fuzzy Zoeller hosted a fishing program on ESPN called *Kmart Outdoors Show*. Knowing my love of fishing, Joe Strasser got me invited to appear on an episode, shot in the deep waters of the Atlantic Ocean, off the coast of Panama, along with NFL player Walter Payton. During this show I landed the biggest fish I have ever caught—a three-hundred-pound black marlin.

You should have seen the one that got away, though! I lost a massive fish, which was at least five hundred pounds, when the line broke after I had been fighting it for over an hour. It was huge.

Walter was hilarious, very animated, and one of the nicest people I have ever met. He got seasick and couldn't take the motion, so we had to take him back to shore. Fuzzy was awesome. Lisa went with us. She got to watch, but she had to stay behind the camera.

Richmond, Virginia

My time in Richmond was very short-lived, only about three weeks. I stayed at a hotel the whole time and never really got a feel for the city.

Nashua, New Hampshire

I lived in a hotel in Nashua, and as I've said, I loved Holman Stadium, the terrific old ballpark. George Toma, the famous groundskeeper from Kansas City, took care of the field one of the summers I played there. Known as "the Sodfather" and "the God of Sod," he was an awesome guy, and it was a thrill to meet someone who took such great pride in every detail of his job.

Albuquerque, New Mexico

Most of my career was played east of the Mississippi River, but in 2000, I signed with the Los Angeles Dodgers and was sent to their Triple-A team in Albuquerque.

New Mexico was gorgeous, people there enjoyed the outdoors, and I loved looking at the Sandia Mountains every day. As I was leaving Boston for Albuquerque, Lisa was flying to Sydney, Australia, to work for NBC at the Olympics as a producer and editor. I remember missing her, but also being extremely proud of her.

Norfolk, Virginia

In Norfolk, Lisa and I lived in an apartment for a very short time, only about three weeks—then I got traded and we packed up and moved to Pawtucket.

Jupiter, Florida

I spent a few days with the Montreal Expos Single-A team in Jupiter, Florida, on an injury rehab assignment.

Nashville, Tennessee

I lived with three of my teammates in Nashville. I fished every day on the lake near our condo. Most of the other guys played golf, but I never brought my clubs. Fishing had a way of relaxing me, restoring energy before or after a game, whereas golf took something out of me, so I never liked to play golf during a baseball season.

Columbus, Ohio

After arriving in Columbus from Nashua, I lived with Lisa's cousin Josh and his wife, Julie. I have good memories of Columbus, including how passionate the people there are about Ohio State University, and their beloved Ohio State Buckeyes sports teams. My daughter, Noelle, is currently a student at Ohio State University, where I have attended a couple Buckeye football games, experiencing the passion of the fans firsthand.

New York, New York

New York was the twentieth city I played in, but it felt like my career was beginning, as if I hadn't really played baseball until I suited up in the famous pinstripes at baseball's ultimate cathedral.

The Yankees put me at the Roger Smith Hotel and I took the subway to the Bronx. Before my first game as a Yankee, I took the obligatory tour of Monument Park, marveling at the history of the franchise. I just wanted to get an opportunity to help the Yankees win a game, and that would be my monument. If I could do that, deep down I'd know I had played a small part in the history of baseball's most famous franchise. Little did I know that in my first game, I would hit a home run to seal a big win over Boston. It was a moment I will never forget.

A day later, I had another memorable moment in the Bronx when, with the bases loaded in the bottom of the ninth inning of a 1–1 tie with Boston, I hit a sharp grounder to second that enabled Hideki Matsui to score from third base, for a walk-off win. There is nothing like experiencing your Yankee teammates pour out of the dugout to mob you after your at bat resulted in a walk-off win over an archrival.

Anaheim, California

When my old friend Bill Stoneman from Montreal, then the general manager of the Angels, signed me to a contract from Nashua in 2004, I became what is believed to be the only player to battle back to the big leagues from an independent-league team on two separate occasions.

I lived in a Homewood Suites hotel, in Anaheim, only a few blocks away from the fantasy world of Disneyland. I didn't know it at the time, but my baseball fantasy life was nearing its end as well.

Salt Lake City, Utah

A year later, the Angels sent me to their Triple-A affiliate, the Salt Lake Bees, in Salt Lake City. Park City, Utah, is only a half hour away from Salt Lake City, and the first time I visited the resort town, I knew I had to live there. In Anaheim, I was living minutes from Disneyland, but to me, Park City was the ultimate fantasyland. I liked it so much, I bought a condo and commuted to the ballpark.

It was about a thirty-minute drive, up and down winding hills, but there was such beautiful scenery that the drive was very relaxing. Sometimes it would be snowing in Park City, but by the time I got to Salt Lake City, it would be clear and dry.

My condo was close to the Provo River, one of the best trout-fishing rivers in the country. I fished every day before the game and was on top of the world. Park City turned out to be one of my favorite places because of my love for the outdoors, and there is so much to do there. I lived across the street from the Olympic ski jump area, and part of me was tempted to try it out, or at least hit the slopes. After I got to the big leagues, I stopped skiing because it is forbidden in MLB contracts, but now that I'm no longer a player, I'm itching to go back to Utah so I can hit the slopes. I'll probably pass on the ski jump.

Little Rock, Arkansas

After the majesty of Utah and the wide-open spaces of the west, Little Rock was a big change of pace. I enjoyed the city, which sits right on the Arkansas River and was experiencing a renaissance, but I didn't have the best experience.

Jose Arredondo was a relief pitcher on our team with a live arm, but he was a crazy guy, disrespectful to the game. We had a huge lead one night when Bobby Magallanes, our manager, brought Jose in to mop up. It was not a save situation, so Jose was not happy. Jose gave up five runs, and Bobby took him out, but before Bobby got to the mound, Jose was on his way to the dugout, clearly violating baseball's unwritten rule that a pitcher stays on the mound to hand the ball to his manager. Then to compound things, Jose just dropped the ball to the ground as he walked past Bobby.

I went off on Jose in the dugout, saying, "You don't disrespect the manager." I was a veteran and believed it was my place to tell him. Then Bobby came back into the dugout and went off on Jose also. In the clubhouse after the game, Jose was clearly pissed at me. He kept staring at me, and I finally said, "Let it go." Bobby asked what the problem was, and Jose responded, "Curtis Pride is the problem." Those were words I'd dreaded my entire life. I worked hard so that no one could ever rightfully say them.

Then Bobby totally backed me, saying, "Listen to Curtis. He's played in the big leagues. You haven't." It was obvious that's not what Jose wanted to hear. He immediately came after me, tried to throw a punch, but missed. I went after him and we got in a scuffle, the only one of my entire career. I wanted to teach him a lesson. We got separated, and Jose was suspended for two weeks by the Angels front office and demoted to Single-A.

It was total vindication for me, but more importantly, it was the first time I realized my playing career had given me something of value to pass on to younger players. Sure, I hoped players would be more receptive in the future, but for the first time, I knew I wanted to teach youngsters the right way to play the game.

I could feel my career slipping away, like a car stuck in reverse, but I was starting to envision a life beyond baseball. I had accepted the demotion to Double-A Arkansas because I believed I would be in the lineup every day, but I have no regrets about my time there because it gave me a glimpse of the future. When I finally got called back up to Triple-A in the middle of June, I knew my career was winding down and I was looking forward to what was coming next. I had turf toe surgery, and I could sense my body telling me it was time to slow down. After the surgery, I spent the rest of the season on the disabled list.

When my son, Colten, was born that July, my priorities changed, and I began to think about life after baseball, with my family as the top priority.

WALDORF, MARYLAND

Other than the occasional road game in Baltimore, I had never played professionally in my home state. I was thirty-nine years old, and it seemed fitting that I should wind up my career thirty-nine miles from my hometown. I still had one more move up my sleeve, one more goal to achieve as a player, before I changed my focus to coaching. I wanted to play in the 2008 Summer Olympics in Beijing as part of the United States baseball team, which Davey Johnson was managing.

If I was going to play in the Olympics, I had to be an active player, so I signed on with the Southern Maryland Blue Crabs, making my fourth trip to an independent team. The team's charming ballpark was brand-new, and I lived in a quaint bed-and-breakfast five minutes away, along with Matt Hensley, another former major leaguer. I knew it would be my last year as a player and I wanted to savor everything about the game, but mostly I was trying to stay sharp so I could play in the Olympics. I had been asked to play in an Olympics team qualifying round in 2006, but I couldn't go because I got promoted to the big leagues. I was told to be ready for the next Olympics, that they liked me because of my experience.

I did well in Southern Maryland, with an .801 OPS in eighty-nine games. I was named to the All-Star team and played in the league's midseason All-Star game. But with all my major-league experience, I was the highest-paid player on the team, so for financial reasons the owner decided to release me at the beginning of August. At that point I knew it was over. I wouldn't play professional baseball again and would not be part of the Olympic team.

I never thought I would play for twenty-six teams. When I was drafted, I thought I would play my entire career for the Mets. You think you are going to be like Cal Ripken Jr. or Tony Gwynn. But nowadays playing for one team is extremely rare. Even most of the really great players play for multiple teams.

There is no bad place to play baseball. I enjoyed every minute of my playing career, loved meeting a lot of people and seeing so much of the country. There were a lot of great people rooting for me, a lot of great memories. You never know where baseball will take you, what the game will teach you, or whom you will meet.

The word "journeyman" has a negative connotation in sports, but playing for many different teams never caused me to feel any shame. If anything, I took pride in joining a new club, quickly fitting in, and helping that team win. My two decades of traveling were not planned, but I wouldn't trade them. I was living my dream, and wherever I played, I met friendly, supportive people who played a role in fulfilling that dream.

CHAPTER 21

On-the-Job Training

During my childhood I never imagined the day would come when I would be coaching or managing a team of my own. Those were grown-up jobs, for seasoned baseball people with extensive playing experience, good people skills, and a strong desire to pass on the things they have learned to others. It wasn't until my career as a player was winding down, when I was considering what to do for a post baseball career, that I realized I now possessed those key qualifications for coaching. I gave the game of professional baseball my all for twenty-three years and, in return, it gave me a mastery of the game's core curriculum.

I have always loved baseball, and my days as a professional player left me with definitive beliefs about how the game should be played, how to run a game, and the best way to connect with players. I had the benefit of exposure to some of baseball's greatest minds, which turned out to be the best education I could hope for. I didn't know it as it was happening, but playing for managers such as Bobby Cox and Mike Scioscia was like being enrolled in a master class on how to honor the game's traditions while moving it forward into the analytics era.

After retiring as an active player, I spent sixteen years as the head baseball coach at Gallaudet University, a school for the deaf, in Washington, DC. Often I am asked how I coached a team made up of deaf and hard of hearing players. It's a question I pondered as

I approached my first season as the baseball coach at Gallaudet, and after my careful consideration, the answer seemed obvious: I incorporated what I believe to be the best aspects of the managers I played for over the course of my career, blended those ideas and ideals with my own sensibilities, and came up with a style that is all my own.

The one thing I never considered was making alterations or exceptions because my players were deaf. Just as I responded to managers who did not treat me differently because of my hearing disability, I extended that same respect to my players. I also strived to develop a personal relationship with everyone who played for me, as I believe good communication skills to be the greatest asset a manager or coach can possess.

Bobby Cox was an excellent communicator, maybe the best I was ever around. He took an interest in your family, sincerely asking about them, while keeping them involved as an extension of the team. He was also very honest about playing time and never kept you in the dark. Bobby told you exactly how he was going to use you and why, patiently answering any questions you had about your status on the team.

I am a strong proponent of being prepared, and believing in your system makes it easier to be accountable, be it to your players or the media. When you see managers who are testy or unwilling to explain their rationale for making a move, it is often because they themselves don't fully believe in what they are doing, or what they did during a game. Bobby would explain exactly what he was doing, because he knew exactly why he was doing it, and his explanations always made perfect sense to his players. That's how you earn the respect of your team.

At the same time I have played for managers who would not tell the truth, even though a player would always rather hear it. Bobby always gave it to you straight, and that's why so many players loved playing for him. He cared equally about everyone, be it a superstar or the twenty-fifth man. He never treated anyone like a commodity. Bobby respected them and gave them the flexibility to do whatever they needed to do to get prepared for the game. In my case he instinctively knew to treat me like one of the guys.

My first big-league manager was Felipe Alou, in Montreal, and he taught me a great deal. Felipe loved playing small ball, calling for hit-and-run plays and stealing bases. He was aggressive and that made playing for him a lot of fun. You had to stay on your toes and play hard.

Mike Scioscia was another very aggressive manager, urging you to go from first to third, even if you risked being thrown out. When I was calling the shots at Gallaudet, I understood the value of being aggressive. You have a much better chance of scoring from third base with two outs—a wild pitch, a passed ball, an error, or even a balk is all it takes. Old-school baseball people always say never make the first or last out of an inning at third base, but Mike did not believe in that. He did not care what out you make at third, he wanted you to be aggressive. That kind of approach on the base paths carries over, and you find yourself with the same energy and focus on the field, which is why I tell my team the same thing—don't worry about making the first or third out at third base, just worry about being aggressive.

Joe Torre was one of the most successful managers in Yankees history, and his presence in the dugout made everyone better. Joe was quiet, but I really liked playing for him. He had been an MVP and that always brings with it a level of respect. More importantly, Joe had a great aura of success that seemed to rub off on his players, and he was always in control, almost as if he knew exactly what would happen before it happened.

I also borrowed liberally from my minor-league managers, especially Jim Tracy. Playing for Jim in Harrisburg was one of the best experiences of my career; he was smart and patient, demanding but fair. He was also a very good man, who took an interest in his players as people.

Mike Quade and Steve Swisher were both very good managers who went the extra mile for me. I'll never forget Steve Swisher coming in early, working with me and throwing batting practice to help me get out of my slump. Steve was probably more frustrated with my initial failing in Double-A than I was. He saw something in me and knew I had a lot of talent and took it personally when I struggled. It was as if my failures were his failures and my success was his success. Watching Steve take a personal stake in the success of the team and the individuals was one of my great lessons for managing.

It's a style that cannot be forced or faked, but rather must come from within. When I was the head coach at Gallaudet, I relied heavily on analytics and would spend long hours on game preparation and tendencies. There are moments within a game where that data is invaluable, but I believe the hours and days that lead up to those moments are every bit as important. I think the time and sweat you spend preparing your players, building relationships with them, establishes the foundation of a team that, in turn, enables you to make the right decision when you are running a game. More importantly, it prepares your players to execute those maneuvers.

If you have treated your players with respect, shown them that you are invested in their success, they will be invested in your success and the success of the team, and your chances of winning increase significantly.

CHAPTER 22

Role Model: My Father

Playing professional baseball for more than two decades allowed me to work alongside numerous teammates who were inducted into the Hall of Fame. Yet, for all the Hall of Famers I have learned from, no one taught me more—no one has been a better role model for me—than my own father.

John Pride was born in 1940 in Youngstown, Ohio, a mostly industrial city located just a few miles from the Pennsylvania state line. His parents, James and Lensie Pride, had moved there in the late 1930s from a small town in Alabama. Having grown up in the Deep South under a system of strict racial segregation, my dad's parents yearned for a better life and expanded opportunities for their future children. In the 1930s, Youngstown was a city of approximately 175,000 people, and opportunities abounded for members of all races in the various steel mills located there. At that time Youngstown was the third-largest steel-producing city in the entire United States, trailing only Pittsburgh, Pennsylvania, and Birmingham, Alabama.

My paternal grandfather worked for over twenty years as a boiler operator at Republic Steel, before retiring on disability in the mid-1950s. My paternal grandmother worked for almost thirty years in the housekeeping department at the JCPenney Company. Although neither of them finished high school, they were both determined that they would find a way for their children to attend college. My father told me that every time he saw his dad walking out the door, carrying his lunch box and heading for work in the hottest part of the steel mill, he was even more convinced he'd be going to college. Similarly, while other fathers in Youngstown were happy to get their teenage sons summer jobs in the mill, my grandfather swore that neither of his two sons would ever set foot in a steel mill.

True to his parents' dreams, my father graduated from Capital University in Columbus, Ohio, in 1963, and his brother, now deceased, graduated from Ohio State University and the Howard University School of Law. While earning his degree at Capital University, my father was also a standout athlete in basketball and track-and-field, and he was inducted in 2001 into the Capital University Athletic Hall of Fame.

After graduating from Capital University in '63, my dad moved to Washington, DC, where his first full-time position was as a police officer with the United States Capitol Police. At that time the Capitol Police force was still partially segregated, as African-American officers could only work in the part of the Capitol Building that housed the U.S. Senate, and not the area where the U.S. House of Representatives is located. This archaic policy changed while my father worked there, primarily through the intervention of Senator Ted Kennedy, of Massachusetts. In fact, my mom's two brothers then followed my dad to the Capitol Police force, and Ronald, her older brother, became the first African-American sergeant and lieutenant in the history of the U.S. Capitol Police.

After about three years with the U.S. Capitol Police, my father decided that he wanted to use his education and skills in a way that could help promote social justice. In 1966, then, he took the federal civil service exam, and because of his high score, my father had the choice of various jobs with several federal government agencies. To him, a position where he felt he could best promote the cause of social justice was a no-brainer. He accepted a position in August 1966 as a civil rights advisory specialist with the United States Department of Health, Education and Welfare (HEW), the precursor to Health and Human Services. Over the course of his career, he worked under eight presidents: Lyndon Johnson, Richard Nixon, Gerald Ford, Jimmy Carter, Ronald Reagan, George H.W. Bush, Bill Clinton, and George W. Bush.

My father became an expert on deafness so that he and my mother could give me the tools that would enable me to develop into my best self. He was there to support me at virtually every game I played as I grew up, which is no small thing when your son is trying over a half-dozen different sports, searching for the one that is his calling. My father did all those things, but I think the best illustration of the man's essence comes by way of one simple story.

During his two-and-a-half years as a compliance officer for the Department of Education, my father was assigned to the state of Mississippi, where he was responsible for investigating and assessing Title VI of the 1964 Civil Rights Act, which denied federal funds to public school systems that did not implement effective desegregation plans.

Simply put, the dual school systems essentially prolonged segregation, creating separate schools for whites and Blacks. My father's job with the Department of HEW was to go to the Deep South to document the continued existence of these dual school systems, and to report whether an honest effort was being made to desegregate these schools. In those cases where they were still maintaining the dual school system, and not trying to abolish it, his reports served as the basis for initiating an administrative hearing to terminate federal funds.

This was the late 1960s, right about the time I was born, and almost all the school systems in the Deep South had implemented what they called Freedom of Choice Segregation Plans. In accordance with the plan, every student was given a "choice form," prior to the beginning of the school year. Their parents would sign the form, stating that they voluntarily chose to attend a certain school.

So, at least theoretically, every student, Black or white, had the opportunity to choose the school they wanted to attend. But in terms of implementing it, there was a great deal of coercion and intimidation—both economic and physical—on Black families. So much so, that virtually no Black family opted to attend a previously all-white school for fear of physical or economic intimidation.

When a Black family did demonstrate the courage to choose a previously all-white school, very bad things would happen to that family. My father saw bullet holes in the walls of houses belonging to families that chose to select a previously all-white school under the Freedom of Choice desegregation plan. Consequently those plans failed, and it was my father's job to document the fact they didn't work because of coercion and intimidation.

He would take affidavits from families, detailing how their houses were shot at, or how they were terminated from jobs after they opted to have their children attend one of the previously all-white schools. The offending school system was then given the opportunity for a hearing in lieu of immediate termination of their funds.

The sight of my father—an educated, authoritative Black man, in a suit and tie, whose mission was to enforce desegregation—was not a welcome one in the Deep South.

My father conducted countless hearings and actually wound up with some terminations, but as the times changed and the late 1960s became the early 1970s, he saw school systems start to come around and use different types of desegregation plans. Eventually, for the most part, schools in the Deep South desegregated and came into compliance with Title VI.

However, getting the last holdouts to comply did not come easily. My father had some harrowing experiences along the way. "There were a lot of times," he told me, "when I was scared to death, times I thought something very bad was going to happen to me."

There are numerous stories he has told me about those days, but I will share just a couple. My father and his team had long been told not to let the sun set on their backs in Neshoba County. It was advice he reluctantly took to heart, typically watching the late-afternoon sun as if its presence in the sky kept him safe by shining an unrelenting light on the abhorrence of racism. As kids we were all told to be home when the streetlights came on, to be safe from the mythical boogeyman. In his job representing the U.S. government, my father was told to be inside when the sun went down, to be safe from very real, very dangerous racists.

On this day, he was interviewing families outside of Philadelphia, Mississippi, and it started to get late. Philadelphia, Mississippi, is the small town where on June 21, 1964, three young civil rights workers Andrew Goodman, James Earl Chaney, and Michael Schwerner disappeared and were later found to have been brutally murdered by several members of the local Ku Klux Klan.

As the warmth and transparency of the sun began to wane, my father knew it was time to get back to the sanctuary of his hotel room in Meridian. The lawyer who was riding with him, Steve Shotkin, and my father decided to take a shortcut back to Meridian. They were driving along a country road, shrouded by sweeping magnolia trees so magnificent they could block out the late afternoon sun and play tricks on your internal clock. Before they knew what happened, darkness had enveloped them.

As they turned a corner, the narrow road they traveled was blocked by a pickup truck. Several men were standing alongside it with rifles. There was no warning and no way my father and Steve could turn around, so they stopped, certain it was all over for them. Neither my father nor Steve said a word. Instead, they just waited in silence, fearing the worst, as one of the guys, gun in hand, inspected their car. Then the gunman looked at my dad and Steve and, without a word spoken, went back to the other guys. After what appeared to be a time lapse of dramatic proportions, one of the gunmen got in the truck, pulled it off the road, and let my dad and Steve drive on. It turns out, my father and Steve assumed, that the men were merely a group of guys out on a hunting trip.

"Let's get the hell back to Meridian," my father said as he hit the gas pedal on the rental car.

On one of the occasional reviews in Alabama to which my father was assigned, a strange thing happened. In the small Alabama town of Opelika—which is less than thirty miles from where my paternal grandmother was born—my father and three of his associates decided to stop for lunch at a small diner. It was four people—two white and two Black—merely looking for a bite to eat in the middle of a workday.

My dad told me he could feel stares the moment he stepped through the spring-loaded screen door into the small restaurant. He and his three colleagues, respectful and well mannered, decided to sit at a back table, where their presence couldn't possibly offend anyone. Soon a waitress came over. This was good. She glared at my father's team, as if daring them to stay. This was not good. Finally the waitress grabbed a pencil from behind her ear, pulled a notepad from her apron, and looked at one of my father's associates.

"May I take your order?"

Hallelujah.

This was not *The Twilight Zone,* nor a reality-TV show where producers intentionally threw opposites together, hoping for an explosion. No, this supposedly was just lunch. Maybe all the hostility had been imagined, my father and his colleagues expecting the worst after hearing too many stories and watching too many newsreels of Freedom Fighters met with unprovoked violence in these parts. So they went ahead and placed their orders.

In a silence you could hear, the group then waited for their meals. The longer it took, the more unsure they became. Would they be allowed to eat, or would they end up being someone else's lunch? With tension in the diner now fomenting like the thick, sultry Southern air, the waitress finally returned and placed sandwiches in front of my father and his one associate who also happened to be Black.

A happy ending, everything is going to be okay, my father thought.

We're going to get to eat. Then we will pay our bill and quietly get down the road, feeling a little foolish for allowing our imaginations to play tricks on us, feeling a little bit of shame for believing the worst about the good people of Alabama.

Not so fast, though.

My father and the other Black man waited for the last two people—a white woman and a white man—to get their food. They waited and waited. And waited some more.

"Go ahead and get started," Lloyd Henderson, my father's boss and one of the two white people waiting on their order, implored. But my father wouldn't dream of engaging in what he believed to be bad table manners.

Finally, after about ten more minutes, Lloyd called the waitress over. "Where is our food?" he politely asked.

The waitress looked squarely at Lloyd. Then she pointed at the two Blacks seated at the table, my father and his coworker Goldia Dargan (nee Hodgdon). "There's a law that says we got to feed them," she said. "But there ain't no law that says we got to feed the white folks who came with them."

At that point my dad's coworker said, loud enough for everyone in the restaurant to hear, "We all eat, or no one eats." Then he asked his three colleagues to join him in getting up and walking out the door, to the jeers and catcalls of the locals in the restaurant. My father joined the others in refusing to eat unless everyone was served.

I hate that story and I love that story.

I hate it because it reinforces every horrific stereotype about ignorance and intolerance, laying bare an undeniable truth about our nation's past. My father first told me that story as I prepared to leave home to play minor-league baseball in the Deep South. He wanted me to understand what can happen, to consider how one person's actions affect others, how there is always a good way to handle a bad situation.

I didn't want to believe something like that could still happen in the 1970s, let alone in the late 1980s as I embarked on my baseball career. Today, in my opinion, with the horribly divided nature of our Red State/Blue State nation, it's no less heartbreaking, but much less surprising.

At the same time I love that story because it illustrates the best qualities of my father and demonstrates why he is the man I most want to be like. Courageous, professional, and compassionate—all at a moment in time when those values put his own well-being in very real danger. My father did not hesitate in joining the right people and doing the right thing. Someday, I'm sure, I'll be put in a perilous situation that calls for those same convictions, and when it happens, I'm not sure how I'll respond. But it's nice knowing I've got the right stuff running through my bloodlines.

I've never been one for clichés. Like it or not, my life has taken a unique path, one where most of the timeworn truisms offer little solace or direction. I have had to cut my own path, find my own words, hear a siren call that exists only in my imagination. When you are writing a book about your life, clichés are probably the last thing anyone wants to read. But there is one adage I especially like, one that directly addresses the responsibility you have when you are in a family, part of a team, or reside in the world in general. It sums up a person's essence and the value that person brings to those around him or her: "If you're not part of the solution, you are part of the problem."

My dad spent an additional thirty-five years in the federal government, rising to the highest career rank, before retiring in 2003. During that time he managed a variety of federal programs providing assistance to vulnerable populations, including runaway and homeless youth, low-income families, and people with disabilities.

John Pride has always been part of the solution.

CHAPTER 23

My Mom

To understand how I made it to the big leagues, you must know the impact my mother had on my development. To do that, you must first come to know my mother. She gave up everything to make sure I had what I needed to succeed, but she never felt like she was making a sacrifice.

Sallie Pride was twenty-seven and had a successful nursing career at Soldiers' Home Hospital in Washington, DC, when I was born. She could have been devastated by the diagnosis that her firstborn son was deaf, but she never flinched, never stopped to grieve, never even slowed down.

"You just keep plugging along, doing the best you can at the time," she told me of her unwavering devotion to her deaf son.

I know I take a lot of cues from her, always moving forward, always fighting my way through difficult circumstances, instead of lamenting my bad fortune or ruminating on being dealt a bad hand. My mom walked away from her career, to make sure I had a counselor, teacher, advocate, and cheerleader. I will forever be the beneficiary. All the good she could have done as a nurse was channeled into my upbringing and I don't take that gift lightly.

My mother volunteered to be my primary caretaker, and, like that, her world changed. Suffice it to say, having a deaf child became the driving force in her life. When I was only a little over a year old, my mother took me to the deaf preschool program at Children's

Hospital in Washington, DC. She tells me she was amazed by how alert and focused on the teachers I was at such a young age. Because of my curiosity and desire to learn, my mom always enjoyed accompanying me to the classes. Where that desire for education came from, I have no idea, but I suspect it was inherent. Just a case of me being lucky to have inherited my parents' eagerness.

My mom says I would sit in my high chair, fold my hands, and attentively focus on whatever the teacher would say. I couldn't hear the teachers, of course, but I instinctively knew they were trying to communicate with me, and I wanted to communicate back. All the while, my mother was there to make sure I had the best care. She would drive me to school, sit in on classes, take notes, and then drive me home.

Once I outgrew the program at Children's Hospital, my future development became an even bigger concern for her. She and my father had to decide what was next for me.

My mother has admitted to me there were times she missed her career. Once I got older and had more independence, she thought about returning to nursing. But she realized that while she was away from her profession, working with me, so much about nursing had changed that she practically would have needed to go back to school for a refresher course before returning to the workplace.

At one point she was actually hired for a job and then said, "I don't want to do it again," and didn't go.

But it's not like my mom didn't have a job. I was a handful, and she was very involved in the Parent, Teacher, Student Association (PTSA), and interacting with other parents. Along with my father, she got involved with the Montgomery County Association for Hearing Impaired Children, and she has said that helped her realize what was possible. She also became active in the Alexander Graham Bell Association for the Deaf and Hard of Hearing, a national advocacy association for oral education for the deaf.

By meeting parents of other deaf kids, my mom could see what those children were doing, and that gave her even more confidence and also enhanced her optimism. Both my parents will tell you that as much work as they put into my well-being, it takes a village to raise a deaf child. While placing so much emphasis on me and providing every opportunity for me to integrate myself successfully into the hearing world, my mother also had my sisters, Jacqui and Christine, to raise.

Both Jacqui and Christine were always knee-deep in extracurricular activities, too. Girl Scouts, gymnastics, softball, and pom-pom squad were some of their favorites, most of which required extensive after-school practice time. They also had a lot of overnighters and sleepovers. How my mom found time for everyone is beyond me.

Two-and-a-half years older than me, Jacqui sacrificed a lot. I think my deafness was probably tougher on her because she could not get as much attention from my parents as I did. They knew she could do things that I could not do, that she was very self-reliant and strong, but I'm sure there were times when my situation made her life much tougher than it needed to be.

But it made things easier for me. Having Jacqui around was like having my own personal protector. She was good at watching over me, willing to put her own reputation on the line if someone tried to mess with me. She was mature enough to realize her brother was more important than the so-called cool kids. She understood family was more important than her friends and school, and I was the beneficiary of her advanced maturity. I will always be grateful.

My sister Christine was always an advocate, too. When I played in the Arizona Fall League, I was able to pay her back. Christine, who was attending the University of Missouri at the time, came to visit me in Mesa, Arizona, to watch me play. One night we went out to dinner and ended up hanging out with Michael Jordan and Charles Barkley. If she doesn't think her big brother is cool after that—and she doesn't—I give up!

As for my mother, one of the things I think says the most about her came after her kids had all grown up and left the house. One day she was reading a story in the *Montgomery Journal* about a desperate need for African-American foster parents.

"That article just jumped out at me," she told me.

That night my mother managed to convince my father that they had so many blessings in their lives, they owed it to the universe to share them with others. With that, they decided to become foster parents. Leonda was four months old when she joined our family as a foster child. Several years later, my parents adopted her, and she officially became my sister.

My parents subsequently took in another foster child, who, coincidentally, had a hearing disability. The Montgomery County School System had a family that was about to be broken up, and it included a girl with a hearing disability. They knew about me and figured my parents would be willing and able. They were right on both counts. Ivy was four years old when she came to our family as a foster child, staying for three years, until her mother regained custody of her. Ivy's mom died several years later, and my parents now consider themselves to be her parents. She remains an important part of our extended family.

My mom didn't want Ivy's family to be broken up, so she did everything she could to keep them together. There were six siblings and my mom strongly believed they needed to remain together. More than anything, she believed a child needed her and that she and my father could provide a better quality of life for Ivy. It was something she didn't choose to do but, rather, had to do. All her life, my mother has had an innate desire to take care of people.

Without a doubt I wouldn't have the purpose-driven life I have today—married and raising two kids, after sixteen years of helping to mentor young men at Gallaudet University—were it not for my mom's influence in my life.

CHAPTER 24

The People You Meet

So much of what my twenty-three-year career playing professional baseball provided me are things I never could have planned or predicted. Included in that is the incredible number of legends and superstars I met along the way.

Early in my career when I was with the Expos, Kevin Malone, the team's general manager, brought acclaimed director Ron Howard onto the field before a game. Ron, a huge baseball fan who went on to win multiple Academy Awards, Emmys and Golden Globes, was making a movie in Montreal at the time, and meeting him was a great thrill for me. But meeting Ron Howard was just the beginning. After my 1994 season in Ottawa, I was selected to play in the Arizona Fall League, which is a prestigious league for top prospects that begins right after the end of the World Series.

The year 1994 was when Michael Jordan decided to retire from the Chicago Bulls and try his hand at professional baseball. He signed with the Chicago White Sox, who then assigned him to their affiliated team in the Arizona Fall League. As a result the Fall League games, which were usually only attended by family, scouts, and a few fans, suddenly became the focus of the sports world. Every game that Michael was scheduled to play in became a fan and media circus.

To help him relax, Michael decided to host invitation-only pickup basketball games on the off days of the Fall League season at a local gym that was closed to the public. Having heard that I had excelled at basketball in college, Michael quickly added me to his small list of invites. As one of the only three players in the Fall League who had also played basketball at the Division I College level, I usually had the task of trying to guard Michael, and he often would be guarding me when our team had the ball.

Michael played hard during the games, so obviously he was able to do pretty much whatever he wanted to during our matchups. But I did have a few memorable moments, too. In one game with the score tied in a "next basket wins" situation, Michael's teammate Terry Francona—the World Series–winning manager of the Boston Red Sox and longtime manager of the Cleveland Indians—took a three-point shot that missed badly and rebounded out to me. I was able to then drive down the court around a few defenders for a game-winning layup.

Michael was not happy, and he walked up to Terry and said, in all seriousness, "Hey, Terry, just so you know. When the score is tied, I ALWAYS take the last shot." After a short moment of being a little stunned, Terry fired right back, "Yes, Michael, now you know how I feel watching you try to hit a curveball!"

In showing what a good sense of humor he has, along with his incredible competitive spirit, Michael took about two more steps before he realized what Terry had said, and then he started laughing so hard that he doubled over and went to the floor.

I was honored many years after that Arizona Fall League season ended when I was told that after being asked in an interview about his memories of the Fall League, Michael said that meeting me was one of his top highlights. Also, the 1994 Arizona Fall League coincided with the peak of Charles Barkley's career with the Phoenix Suns, so I also hung out several times with Charles. As you can imagine, those were always fun and interesting evenings.

But in no disrespect to Michael or Charles, my most memorable meeting with a sports legend was when I was lucky enough to meet the greatest of all time, Muhammad Ali. Ali visited our clubhouse during Spring Training with the Angels, and I took a picture with him, which hangs on my office wall today. At the time it was kind of sad. Ali had difficulty interacting with us and was unable to say much of anything. Some of my teammates brought their young kids with them to meet the champ. Each player would come over, one by one, and when the kids were with their dad, you could see the smile widen on Ali's face. His assistant said Ali loved children—they would always make him smile.

I told Ali that I loved watching him box, had a ton of respect for him, that he was my idol. He could hear me and understood what I was saying, but could not respond. I still had vivid memories of Muhammad Ali in his prime when he could "float like a butterfly and sting like a bee." Now, here he was, moving slowly if at all, unable to speak. It was heartbreaking and inspirational, all at the same time. It was a reminder that we have a limited amount of time to make an impact on the world, and it was delivered to me by the greatest of all time.

That's the thing about baseball that stays with me the most. The relationships, the friendships, and the chance meetings you have that can change your life forever. Before I established myself as a Major League Baseball player, I was known more for being a good college basketball player, and during the offseasons in Maryland, I was invited to participate in numerous pickup basketball games organized by Cal Ripken Jr. Cal was so dedicated to fitness that he had an indoor basketball court at his house, along with a weight room that would have made a lot of colleges envious.

I was still somewhat awestruck by the level of baseball star power in the games, but Cal always made me feel like I belonged, giving me the opportunity to compete with professional athletes, which bolstered my confidence. More importantly, Cal provided a master class in dedication and professionalism. I watched the way Cal carried himself, the respect he gave pickup basketball games and his fellow competitors.

After going all out in five or so full-court basketball games, Cal would still hit the weight room. As evidenced by his incomparable

Iron Man streak of 2,632 consecutive big-league games played, Cal never cheated baseball, the fans, or himself. I wanted to be known for the same attributes, and with Cal, I had the living embodiment to watch and learn from. Looking back, I realize it came at a pivotal time in my career.

Later in my life, after I had retired from playing professional baseball, I had the opportunity to work directly for several years with President Barack Obama and First Lady Michelle Obama, which I will talk about in more detail later in the book.

During my childhood my goal was always to play big-league baseball. But the experiences I had, and the people I met on the road to that end, turned out to be an even bigger reward—none more than a chance meeting with David Van Sleet.

I have never viewed my hearing disability as a defining characteristic, but I am not stupid; I know others do. My deafness is often the feature that makes me stand out in a crowd. It can cut both ways, bringing scorn or celebration, fame or infamy, heartbreak or hope. Some people are inspired by it, others are afraid of it.

Over time, however, I have reached a place where I view my deafness as something that brings only perspective and gratitude. It makes me feel grateful that I am faced with a challenge I can handle, one that has enabled me to understand there are many people facing far greater challenges. There can also be feelings of guilt that my disability sometimes brings with it special treatment or sympathy, the kind of attention I do not invite, the kind I do not believe is appropriate for my situation.

All that leaves me with an understanding of what it's like to go through life being judged by something I don't have, as opposed to being appreciated for what I do possess. Thus, I carry with me a desire to share my experience with people who live their lives in similar circumstances, to extend a hand to those who need it most. I have been the recipient of outreach from so many wonderful people, I've always felt a need to repay the favor.

It's not anything I deserve praise for, because it is more of a primal need, something I must do, as opposed to something I choose to do. I have no doubt it is, at least partly, a residual effect of being raised by my parents. It was during my playing career that I first had the opportunity to spend time with deaf and hard-of-hearing kids and their parents, and it brought such great joy that it left me hungry for more.

Raising Noelle and Colten with Lisa, and revitalizing the baseball team at Gallaudet, has brought me to the realization sharing the lessons I have learned is the most rewarding aspect of my life. Frankly, I didn't think I had room for any additional parenting, mentoring, or coaching.

Then I met David Van Sleet.

David and I were competing on opposing sides in a celebrity softball game after a Washington Nationals game at Nationals Park. I was playing outfield for the celebrity team made up of former pro athletes and local media personalities, while David was coaching our opponents, a team made up of Louisville Slugger Warriors—military veterans who had been injured, often severely, in battle. David was the president and general manager of the Louisville Slugger Warriors softball team, which then became the Louisville Slugger Warriors National Amputee Baseball Team after I agreed to become head coach. We then began competing in the Men's Senior Baseball League (MSBL) tournaments hosted by league founder Steve Sigler, father of actress Jamie-Lynn Sigler, who portrayed Meadow Soprano on HBO's *The Sopranos*.

The sight of amputees turning silky smooth double plays, hurling perfectly placed strikes, and men who had been caught in explosions, which could have destroyed their spirits, playing with the passion and pure joy of a Little Leaguer, was all too much. The spirit and skill of this group made the Louisville Slugger Warriors National Amputee Baseball Team the most amazing baseball team I had ever seen play. They made my predicament, with only a hearing disability to overcome, feel like I'd gotten a huge break, as if I, and not Lou Gehrig, was "the luckiest man on the face of the earth." They also made me feel something else; they made me feel like this was a team I had to somehow be a part of.

David himself is one of the most accomplished individuals I have ever met. He is an army veteran, with a degree in prosthetics from George Mason University, a man who managed all the prosthetic programs in Virginia and the Southwest, while specializing in eyes. David is a pioneer in the field, using dental materials to create and rebuild eyes and eye sockets, which are both artistically appealing and technically sound. He started the Louisville Slugger Warriors softball team, and managing it became his hobby. David and I hit it off immediately that night at Nationals Park, and I was so impressed with his team that I invited him and a couple of his players to speak to the team I was coaching at Gallaudet.

A day later, David and two of his players were at Gallaudet, giving my team a presentation, the likes of which they would never forget. His talk was powerful, his words both sobering and incredibly inspirational at the same time.

The players were deeply affected by David's visit. It opened their eyes and made them realize they really didn't have much to complain about. I believe they became much more appreciative of the things they had, including the opportunity to play baseball while also getting a top-flight college education at Gallaudet.

Two years later, David asked me to coach the Louisville Slugger Warriors National Amputee Baseball Team that was headed to Japan to compete in the international World Series for the Physically Challenged. David believed I would be a perfect fit because I could relate to having a disability, and I wouldn't feel any pity toward the players. He was right about the second part; it's hard to feel pity when you are feeling so much awe. As for relating to the players, he was wrong about that part. What those players do far outweighs anything I had to go through due to my deafness.

A small part of me wanted to know what it felt like to see people who had been dealt an even tougher hand than I had been, and yet still overcame that challenge and became successful. This team gave me something very few people could.

Playing in Japan had always been on my bucket list, so when this opportunity arose, it was as if there were some sort of divine intervention at work. We began with a two-day training camp in Estero, Florida. During the camp we took what had been a softball team and converted it to a baseball team. I brought Will Chapman, one of my former players at Gallaudet, who is deaf. You are allowed one player with a hearing disablity; the rest of the team must be made up of players with physical disabilities. The players made the transition from softball to baseball with ease, as if they were born to play hardball, which, in a manner of speaking, they were.

A month later, we reconvened and flew to Osaka, Japan. There we took a two-hour bus ride into the mountains near Kobe. The guys were very excited, and, in turn, so was I. There is nothing more infectious than a passionate team, on a road trip together, counting on one another. Japan was the heavy favorite; they had never lost a single game in all three tournaments they had previously hosted.

In the final game we sent Matt Kinsey to the mound, one of the players who had spoken so eloquently to my team at Gallaudet. Matt, it turns out, wasn't all talk. He turned in one of the gutsiest performances I have ever witnessed. Matt had played college baseball before losing his right leg from the ankle down while serving in the army. Matt pitched a shutout and we beat Japan in the final, 5–0, to hand them their first defeat in four years and win the tournament.

In the fall of 2018, I coached the team again in the Men's Senior Baseball League World Series in Phoenix, Arizona. Anytime David calls, I will answer. I love being around the team because they have fun, play hard, and never complain. It's everything baseball is supposed to be. We played ten games in five days in Phoenix, which amounted to eighteen innings each day. That kind of grind is tough on able-bodied players, but for amputees, it's nearly impossible. Yet, not one word of complaint was spoken by a player.

I knew they were hurting, but they wouldn't tell me. Toward

the end of the tournament, you could see they were tiring, but they kept plugging away. They battled through and finished second in the tournament, but I felt like the big winner. We were the only team made up of players with disabilities in this able-bodied tournament, yet we still made it all the way to the championship game.

When I retired from baseball, I felt a void because I never played in the World Series and did not achieve my goal of playing in Japan. The Louisville Slugger Warriors filled that gap and much more, giving me a gift I cannot repay. Really, it should come as no surprise. Giving gifts they know can never be repaid is what their lives are all about.

CHAPTER 25

He's No Dummy

Every time I took the field to coach the young men at Gallaudet University, I was reminded that I'm not so much a pioneer as I am a torchbearer for deaf baseball players. Gallaudet played its games on Hoy Field, named after William Ellsworth "Dummy" Hoy, the first great deaf major leaguer, a fact that was—and remains—an enormous source of inspiration to me.

Hoy wasn't just the Deaf community's Jackie Robinson, he was its Babe Ruth, Ted Williams, Mickey Mantle, and any other transformative star you can name. During a fourteen-year major-league career, from 1888 to 1902, Hoy hit .288 with forty home runs, 725 RBIs, and 596 stolen bases. A center fielder, Hoy played for seven teams, with his most productive years coming in a Cincinnati Reds uniform, which he wore during two separate stints.

William Hoy was dubbed "Dummy" because he did not speak. At that time there was nothing derogatory about the nickname, but rather it was a literal description of his most prominent feature, like calling someone with a slight build "Slim," or someone with red hair "Red." It wasn't clever, but it wasn't offensive, either.

I have been called "Dummy" on more than one occasion, and when it happens, it comes with malice. Stupid, idiot, numbskull, retard, spaz, and the ever-popular Helen Keller have all been used to address me, and when it happens, I take great offense. But I don't show it.

To react to these taunts would mean losing control. It would also mean giving them credence, so I take a moment and let them sail over my head, just as I would a wild, unhittable pitch. It's never easy, and it's taken me years of practice, self-discipline, and, most importantly, self-confidence, but I would rather let my diction and intellect slowly win you over instead of delivering a verbal knockout punch by lowering myself to the level of someone who must resort to such low-level name-calling.

Hoy was able to ignore the naysayers to blaze his own path, and part of what made him so inspirational to me was his unique road to big-league success. After graduating from the Ohio School for the Deaf, Hoy worked as a cobbler, repairing shoes for a living, and playing baseball for fun on the weekends. Hoy stood just five-four, but his speed caught the eye of a scout, who signed him to play for Oshkosh in the Northwestern League. He reached the big leagues in 1888, leading the National League with eighty-two stolen bases while playing for the old Washington Nationals.

It would be ninety-four years between his retirement and my full season with the Tigers in 1996, and while I can't say for sure why it took so long, I do have my theories. During most of that gap, aspiring deaf players had no active role models to provide inspiration or a road map. They also had to contend with the sort of stay-in-your-lane mentality that I always found defeatist.

Often, it's the self-imposed obstacles that are the hardest to clear, but there were also outside barriers to hurdle, a kind of institutional bias, which was mostly the result of a lack of education. It was easy for general managers, managers, coaches, and players to be afraid of a deaf player because they had never encountered one before. The natural inclination was to believe a deaf player would make their lives more difficult. They would have to slow down to communicate with me and that downshift might bring about damage to their own careers.

I am a baseball player and coach by trade, but part of my job is to educate people about the Deaf community and their ability to assimilate. I've always believed the best way to teach is by demonstration, so rather than offering a lecture that explained to people that I could be a good teammate, I've always chosen to show it. If I didn't make a big deal of my deafness, I believed, others wouldn't, either.

Despite the fact that there was nearly a century between Dummy Hoy and me, I always considered him a muse. It was an honor to coach on a field named for him.

Hoy was born with hearing before a bout with meningitis at the age of three robbed him of much of his ability to hear. By the time of his affliction, Hoy had already begun to develop a vocabulary, but he did not become an oralist; instead he learned sign language. Without question, learning to talk was my greatest challenge because I had never heard words, and those who deal with deafness later in life do not have to contend with the intense speech therapy I went through. I believe the path I took was more challenging, but it was worth all the hard work.

Being born deaf had an upside: It meant I never had to deal with the trauma of sudden deafness—although my parents went through the turmoil of learning their newborn son could not hear—and I have never known a world other than one in which I cannot hear. To me, my life is completely normal, although not without its challenges.

Having his hearing until age three, Hoy's challenges, conversely, were sudden and traumatic. In addition to being a trailblazer for the Deaf community, Hoy changed baseball for everyone. Because he could not hear the home plate umpire calling balls and strikes, hand signals were introduced. Hoy would make it a point to look back at the umpire after every pitch to get the ball or strike call. I did the same thing throughout my career, mostly because I didn't always trust the scoreboard to be accurate, but also in tribute to Hoy. Umpires always treated me fairly, and if I ever got a bad call, I knew it had nothing to do with my deafness.

Just as Hoy's deafness had a permanent effect on baseball with home plate umpires using hand signals to call balls and strikes, there is the possibility that my ability to read lips also contributed to a baseball tradition.

In today's game, whenever there is a conference between a pitcher and a coach on the mound, the pitcher and other players will shield their mouths with their baseball gloves when speaking. It's a fairly recent phenomenon in the long history of baseball.

In July of 2022, Daniel Brown wrote an article that appeared in *The Atlantic* tracing the history of the tactic. Multiple theories are considered, including one espoused by Greg Maddux, the Hall of Fame pitcher, as reported by Brown.

"... Maddux said the bigger reason for the coverage and widespread usage around the league was Curtis Pride, an outfielder ... who broke in with the Montreal Expos in 1993 ... Pride was a fluent lip reader, and Maddux says that pitchers around the league were well aware of that."

Maddux was quoted in Brown's piece that ran in *The Atlantic*: "When Pride was with Montreal, he could read lips from the dugout if pitchers didn't cover their mouths. So that's kind of where it started. That was my take on it. I remember my brother (Mike) told me about that. When I started (covering my mouth), I started doing it because of Curtis Pride."

Obviously, I don't know if Greg's version of why that tradition has become a widespread part of baseball is the correct one, but coming from an eight-time All-Star and four-time Cy Young Award winner, I'm certainly willing to go with it.

Given the level of apprehension I faced from baseball people in the late 1980s and early 1990s, I can only imagine the burden Hoy must have carried back in the late 1880s. I had the benefit of a century of evolution and development, yet I still had to deal with my share of ignorance and disrespect from a segment of fans, opponents, and, on occasion, even teammates.

Those experiences gave me a greater appreciation for what Jackie Robinson went through when he broke the game's color barrier in 1947. While I didn't experience anything close to what Jackie went through, I have so much respect for him because I got a small taste of discrimination and ignorance. Even now, as a grown man with a family and a place in the community, I cross paths with cruel people. I've learned you must have thick skin, be mentally strong, and not care what other people think or say. If you let people detract from you, you won't be successful. These are simple lessons you learn in grade school, but in my case they are lessons that took decades for me to absorb fully.

While most fans were supportive, I never got too comfortable in the outfield, always keeping my guard up, because it wasn't entirely uncommon for someone to give me a hard time. When you are playing in stadiums that hold upward of fifty thousand fans, it was almost inevitable that there would be one in every crowd. When I was with the Braves, playing right field at old Three Rivers Stadium in Pittsburgh, fans started throwing hot dogs at me. They littered right field with hot dogs. Manager Bobby Cox called us in, off the field. Three or four groundskeepers had to go clean up the hot dogs. I still don't know what the significance of the hot dogs was. Maybe they thought I was a hot dog because I was not responding to their words. Maybe they thought because I was deaf and playing in the big leagues, I was showing off.

But showing off, styling, profiling, flexing as they sometimes call it in the big leagues, was never my way. From the first time I stepped on the field, I was determined to let my game show people what I was all about. That was a way to honor Dummy Hoy and deaf people everywhere.

Playing the game the right way and never disrespecting the game, or its long history, were always the guiding principles for me throughout my long career.

CHAPTER 26

Follow Your Heart

Throughout my life I have been surrounded by good, hardworking, successful people. It has been one of my great blessings, giving me strong role models who exhibit positive behavior that is worth emulating.

It was only after I left home and made my way through the minor leagues, where I was surrounded by teammates who repeatedly succumbed to temptation, that I realized how fortunate I had been. So very often, making the right choice was simply a matter of mimicking the kind of decisions that had already been made by my family members, friends, teachers, and mentors.

Being away from home for the first time, making new friends from different backgrounds, made me realize that what often feels like second nature to me can be a great challenge to others. Don't misunderstand, I've made plenty of mistakes and I wrestle with difficult decisions, like anyone else; but having seen others go through similar trials and tribulations, only to come out stronger on the other side, has always helped me through challenging times.

One of the biggest decisions I made—with the input and support of my parents—was choosing to attend a mainstream school. Beyond that, the next most important choice I made was to pursue a life in baseball. When I graduated from William & Mary, I had the option of leaving the game in order to pursue a career in finance.

While I believed I had the education and innate skills to be successful in the business world, it wasn't in my heart.

Finance would have been an easier road for me, without as many twists and turns, but I wasn't passionate about it. I loved baseball, and while I had no guarantee of ever getting anywhere near the major leagues, I elected to pursue my dream rather than play it safe. It's a decision I have never regretted or second-guessed.

There have been plenty of times when I was frustrated, when I felt I wasn't reaching my true potential, or when I believed baseball wasn't ready for a deaf player, moments when I thought I wasn't getting a fair shake. But I never doubted my career choice and always viewed those bumps in the road as if they were the ups and downs on a very thrilling carnival ride—one that only the brave, or crazy, dare climb aboard.

I always had the luxury of knowing I had an education, and if things ever got dicey, I could switch gears and take the more conventional career route. That was the gift my parents gave me by insisting I go to college every offseason during my first four years of professional baseball. It's funny, while education was giving me something to fall back on, it was also giving me the confidence to help ensure I kept moving forward and never needed to fall back on anything.

When I talk to young people, regardless of whether they have a hearing disability or not, I urge them to get the best education possible. Then I tell them to find their true passion and pursue it with everything they have. My dream was always to make it to the major leagues. One at bat in the majors might have initially satisfied me, but once I achieved that goal, I realized I wanted more, so I managed to squeeze twenty-three seasons of professional baseball out of a body many considered broken at birth. By the time I played my final game, I knew America's pastime was more than that to me. Baseball, I realized, was more than a game, more than a job. Baseball was a way for me to fit in: a meritocracy where results trumped all else. If you could play, you belonged.

At that point I knew I was a baseball lifer. Somehow the baseball gods must have known it, too. How else can you explain Gallaudet University reaching out to me to coach their baseball team right at the time my playing days were ending? And how do you explain the Major League Baseball Commissioner's Office calling me out of the blue in 2016 and appointing me Ambassador for Inclusion? Or the president of the United States asking me to serve on the President's Council on Fitness, Sports & Nutrition?

I have been blessed by baseball and I truly believe it's because I gave the game my all. The game, in turn, is rewarding me. I was never offered a multimillion-dollar contract and will never be inducted into the Baseball Hall of Fame, two things I always wanted. Instead, baseball has given me what I needed. I represent Major League Baseball to ensure everyone will have the same opportunities I had. Ideally, doors will be open for all.

For several summers, when I was not coaching at Gallaudet, I traveled to big-league cities to meet with the clubs under the leadership of the MLB Department of Diversity, Equity and Inclusion (DEI). We worked together to find ways to be more inclusive, which can mean creating greater accessibility in every stadium, or finding ways for teams to build bridges with their local community. We did programs for children with disabilities. In my travels I met with everyone: the stadium director, the community relations director, marketing officials, and attorneys. Basically, I worked with a team's different departments to cover as many different bases as possible. One day, I believe, those club executives will be made up of more minorities and people with disabilities.

It was work I really enjoyed, probably because I believe it is so important. It's a long process, but we are moving in the right direction. The goal is to make Major League Baseball the most inclusive and accessible of all the major sports.

One of the great honors of my life was serving for six years on President Barack Obama's Council on Fitness, Sports & Nutrition. Like so many of my life's rewards, this appointment came like a lightning strike, completely unexpected and soul-stirring. I was thrilled to work for President Obama, and it was another example of the baseball gods smiling down on me, presumably for a life of dedication to the game. There is no other way to explain it.

As a member of the council—which also included sports legends Michelle Kwan, Dominique Dawes, Drew Brees, Billie Jean King, Grant Hill, Chris Paul, Carl Edwards, and Allyson Felix—we would conduct events at elementary schools, set up exercise stations, and talk about the importance of keeping your body moving. Our country has a huge problem with kids who are overweight, and we spent a great deal of time teaching them about staying active and eating right.

First Lady Michelle Obama took an active role in the council, and I worked closely with her and her fitness organization, Let's Move!, in conducting events to educate children on the benefits of exercise and good nutrition. She was always so gracious and down-to-earth in our interactions—a terrific person and outstanding first lady.

Also, while I was serving on President Obama's Council on Fitness, Sports & Nutrition, I got a call from the White House asking me to be a member of the United States Delegation for the Closing Ceremony of the 2012 Summer Olympics in London, England. As part of the presidential delegation, I joined Susan Rice, Louis Susman, Benjamin Rhodes, Michelle Kwan, and Reginald Love in representing the United States at a number of competitions in London, as well as at the closing ceremonies.

I got the invitation just a few days before I had to leave, and after a mad scramble to coordinate travel arrangements and security clearances with the White House, I embarked on one of the most inspirational trips of my life. I was in London for three days, met with numerous U.S. athletes, and attended the closing ceremony on behalf of the president. I was never prouder to be an American, and after spending several days watching the athletes of the world come together, I was also proud to be a part of the international community as well.

Baseball has been the gift that keeps giving. Just when I thought the game had given me its all, it gave me even more. I tell you these things not to impress you, but rather to impress upon you the unexpected rewards that can come your way when you find what you love and dedicate yourself to giving it everything you have.

That's the best advice I can offer anyone.

Dedicating my life to the game I love has provided me with more blessings than I could have ever imagined, none of which is greater than meeting my wife, Lisa, back at Spring Training in West Palm Beach, Florida. Lisa and I have built the family that is the center of my universe. Lisa is an accomplished journalist, but she has always put family first. She continued her career as a sportscaster after we were married, but left her job following the birth of our daughter, Noelle, in 2004. Three years later, we were blessed with the arrival of our son, Colten.

Noelle and Colten have been the focal point in our lives, and both are good athletes. Noelle excels in basketball and flag football, while Colten is a little like his father in that he is an all-round athlete, playing travel baseball while also participating in basketball and soccer. Watching their games has become a highlight for me and I find myself watching and rooting as if they were participating in the World Series or the WNBA Finals.

Both inherited some of their father's hearing issues. Noelle and Colten being born with varying degrees of hearing loss seemingly disproves the long-held assumption that my own deafness was a result of my mom's bout with rubella while pregnant with me. Now we believe it might be something in my genetic makeup, something that I passed on. Not that it matters. Not to me, anyway. I hope and pray my children feel the same way.

Noelle is a natural athlete and has cochlear implants, which have helped her considerably. Cochlear implants, which were invented in 1957, are a surgically implanted neuroprosthetic device that provides a sense of sound to a person with moderate-to-profound hearing loss. The device bypasses the normal acoustic hearing process and replaces it with electric signals. Those signals stimulate the auditory nerve, and, with training, the brain can learn to interpret those signals as sound and speech.

The devices evolved slowly over the next two decades, and by the mid-1970s, NASA engineer Adam Kissiah developed the modern cochlear implants. The implants, and the science behind them, are so advanced, it literally took a rocket scientist to refine them.

The quality of the sound Noelle hears through her cochlear implants is outstanding, so she has excellent speech. Whereas I had to learn to say words I had never heard, Noelle is able to hear well enough to develop her voice. Noelle can listen to music and talk to people on the phone, things I cannot do.

With cochlear implants, after sound is converted via electric signals, which, in turn, stimulate the auditory nerve, the brain takes over. Much as my brain somehow used the sounds and vibrations of letters to build words and, eventually, an entire vocabulary, the brain of a cochlear implant user adapts to this kind of hearing and interprets the electric signals as sound and speech.

At this point in my life, I don't think cochlear implants would be much help for me. If I were to be fitted for them, it would take at least two to three years to reprogram my brain to the new sound, and it would be like starting all over again. Without the benefit of cochlear implants, I had to learn different tones, the pitch, and sounds I never knew and had never heard. Now that I have developed my speech and mastered the art of reading lips, it would be difficult to throw all that development out the window and start anew.

Colten has some hearing loss in his left ear and has normal hearing in his right ear. He might sometimes have to turn his head a little to listen with his good ear, but hearing is not really an issue for him. We are blessed that our children are healthy and don't really consider minor hearing challenges to be an issue. It's just a normal part of our lives.

CHAPTER 27

Being Heard

Sixteen years ago I drove through the silence of a frigid January morning, winding my Ford Explorer through the icy streets of Washington, DC, en route to the nation's foremost school for the deaf. The road to Gallaudet University is a short forty-minute drive from my boyhood home in Silver Spring, Maryland, but I had never been there.

I have been deaf since birth and I was about to begin my first day as the head baseball coach at Gallaudet University, the only university in the world for deaf and hard-of-hearing students. Because I was born deaf and Gallaudet is a school for the deaf and hard of hearing, you might think I was born to be there, or that I was on some kind of rendezvous with destiny.

I pulled my S.U.V. into the parking lot, and as I walked across the idyllic snow-covered campus that first day, I was more nervous than I was when I walked to home plate to face major-league pitching for the first time. That's because my earliest memories of growing up involve contending with school administrators and teachers who wanted to send me to a school for the deaf. As a child I spoke with a severe speech impediment, which was difficult to understand, but with the help of my parents, I managed to talk my way into a mainstream school with hearing kids.

Sports saved my soul. When I was seventeen, I was one of the most sought-after athletes in the Maryland, Washington, DC, and

Virginia areas, and Gallaudet was among the many colleges that recruited me. But in sports Gallaudet competed only at the Division III level and I knew that I wanted to compete at the highest level of Division I. I understood of course why Gallaudet made an offer and I appreciated it, but I was confident that I was good enough to play anywhere.

When Gallaudet called again years later, things were different. I was hanging on to faded glory with both hands, playing with teammates young enough to be my kids on an obscure independent team called the Southern Maryland Blue Crabs. That's when I got an email from Bob Davila, Gallaudet's president at that time, asking me if I had any interest in coaching the school's baseball team. My best days as a player were long behind me, and I had no idea where my future would lead me, but I never imagined it would be at Gallaudet.

How wrong I was. It took me four decades to realize Gallaudet was precisely the place I needed to be, the place where I could make my biggest impact. So there I was, at thirty-nine, starting all over at the last place in the world I ever expected to be. The last place turned out to be the right place at that time. During my sixteen years as Gallaudet's head baseball coach, I spent the better part of my days working with kids facing the same challenges I overcame to play baseball, on a field where we sometimes had to shovel snow off the field.

The remaining part of those days were spent studying sign language, which is a requirement at Gallaudet. Up until accepting the position there, I hadn't taken the time to learn much more than a rudimentary level of sign language, because I was always focused on improving my oral skills. But while I was working at Gallaudet, I wanted to improve my sign language as much as possible.

I have a wife and two kids in Florida, a college degree, and a résumé that includes parts of eleven years in the big leagues. I've accomplished more than I ever dreamed was possible when I was fighting for a chance in the hearing world. I find it funny that I followed up my playing career doing something I swore I'd never do.

But things change. I'm not the same person I was at seventeen, and the world isn't the same place it was back then, either, certainly not for the deaf or hard of hearing.

When Bob Davila told me he wanted Gallaudet to change right along with the rest of the world, he caught my attention. Bob told me the perception of Gallaudet is not consistent with its reality, and he believed sports could help change the school's identity. Under its then athletic director Mike Weinstock, Gallaudet wanted to make its athletic department more progressive and relevant.

At that moment in time, Gallaudet and I had everything in common. My whole life has been dedicated to using sports to change people's perceptions. So, when Bob told me he wanted Gallaudet to do the same thing, I knew I had to be a part of it. I had something that no one else could offer Gallaudet, and if I didn't take the job, I would be turning my back on the people I could help the most.

The Gallaudet baseball team was coming off a horrendous 4–29 season in which they weren't even competitive, losing twenty-three of their thirty-three games by ten runs or more, including games with scores such as 31–1, 30–2, 23–2, and 20–0. So I knew going in, reviving the program would not be easy. But I also knew if I could turn the baseball team around, I could turn some lives around at the same time. All that would go a long way toward changing the way people view both Gallaudet and deaf people.

That first morning on the job, I called my players into a small classroom in the athletic department. "Things will be different," I told them.

One of my assistant coaches, Ryan Lentz, helped me with the sign language, but the message was all mine. The players focused intently on what I was saying. "If you want people to view you differently," I told them, "you have to start by seeing yourself differently."

I never viewed the deaf kids in my program any differently than the major leaguers I played alongside, and I wouldn't allow my team to view themselves differently, either.

"You are not kids anymore," I said. "You will all be treated like men. And you will be treated the way players who can hear are treated. You need to be committed and pay the price for whatever decisions you make. That's how it works out in the world, and that's how it will work here."

If one of my players showed up late for practice—it didn't matter if it was only five or ten minutes—they ran laps. Tardiness was not tolerated.

"You can't let your hearing disability be an excuse for anything or let it affect your performance," I told them. "That's why communication is so important. You can't afford not to understand, because as soon as you do, someone will say, 'We can't invest in this guy.' You are deaf, so many people already assume you can't cut it. The burden of proving them wrong is on you. You must be twice as good as a hearing player to get half the chance."

Some kids think being deaf or hard of hearing is an excuse to take the lazy way out. But I wanted my players to understand that won't work in this society. They cannot use their deafness as an excuse. Our playing schedule at Gallaudet was made up of hearing schools. Those schools might have had an edge in recruiting, because they had access to two hundred thousand to three hundred thousand high school seniors, compared with the pool of perhaps twenty to thirty high school senior baseball players who are deaf or hard of hearing whom we could go after. But, otherwise, I believe that a hearing team has no advantage over a deaf team.

In my first season we took our lumps, finishing 8–25–1. But by my fourth year, with my coaching philosophies in place, and a team of players I had recruited, we had consecutive seasons of twenty-five wins, twenty wins, and then a school record twenty-seven wins, in which we tied for our league championship and were the number one seed in our conference tournament. I was honored to be named United East Conference Coach of the Year two times, and was thrilled for our players when we defeated five teams ranked in the nation's Top 25, including four in one season.

My team at Gallaudet could compete with any team of hearing players on any playing field. And if you can compete on the baseball field, you can compete in the classroom. And in the boardroom. And everywhere else.

Hearing is not all that important. Trust me, it's not. I've now been deaf for fifty-five years, and I've gotten along just fine, and rarely felt like I was missing out on anything. You can read lips, send text messages, and intuit body language.

Learning to read lips and speak was difficult, but I could do both of those things by the time I was six years old. The desire to make a statement has been a never-ending quest. That's why I spent twenty-three years playing professional baseball in twenty-six different cities. It's why I wouldn't quit when kids made fun of my speech impediment on the Little League fields, and teammates mocked me in the minor leagues. It's why I wouldn't stop dreaming until I made it to the major leagues. And it's why I kept playing until I was thirty-nine, and relegated to an obscure minor-league team, with virtually no shot of ever getting back to the big leagues.

The need to be heard is what fueled me through more than two decades of professional baseball, and it's why I coached at a school for the deaf, the very institution I wanted to avoid in the past. Coaching baseball at Gallaudet gave me a voice, the same way playing Major League Baseball gave me a voice, and being a motivational speaker gives me a voice.

No, hearing isn't a big deal.

The important thing is being heard.

What People Say About Curtis Pride

Curtis didn't let his disability get in the way. I know everybody would always say it's tough for a deaf person to play baseball because there is so much verbal communication, but he saw the game so well that it never became an issue for him. He always went out of his way to learn other players' habits and the things they did on the field, so communication was never a problem. He went above and beyond what he needed to do, and he was successful at it.

I would watch him play and I couldn't tell he had a hearing disability. After a while you get so used to him communicating and talking to him that the only time you knew he was deaf was if you turned your head while you were talking to him.

I think being a point guard in basketball helped him in baseball. He learned to see so much that it never became an issue. People would say, "Maybe he can't hear me call him off," but it never became an issue. He was so good at seeing everything and realizing stuff before it was going to happen that he never got himself in a situation that would inhibit his play.

I think because of his deafness, he really paid attention. You could see on the field that he was always aware of his surroundings and what was going on. He made it a point to always know what was going on. Sometimes in baseball stuff happens behind your back, but he was always in tune with it, and that helped make him a great athlete. He was in the Arizona Fall League, and we'd go play pickup basketball games with Michael Jordan. It was fun. Curtis is a phenomenal athlete. He could do it all. He could play baseball and basketball equally well. Just an extremely talented guy.

In basketball he could elevate the play of the people around him. Being able to handle the ball the way he could, drive the lane and give you a lot of open shots, was awesome. He was really good at setting up plays. He definitely had that gift of elevating a game. Because of not being able to hear, he had to see everything, which is a skill that people sometimes take for granted. He was great at it.

—*Jason Giambi,*
NEW YORK YANKEES TEAMMATE

You don't even think about his deafness. Curtis is so good at reading lips that you don't even think he might not understand what you're saying, because he always gets it. He always managed to put himself in the right spot.

Curtis is fantastic. He is hilarious, he's funny, he jokes around with everybody, and everybody jokes around with him. That's just Curtis. He's no different than anybody else. Obviously, he couldn't hear, but he never made it an issue, so it wasn't one.

Whether you can hear or not has no bearing on whether you can play this game. Curtis Pride proved that. He can play, he can hit, he can run, and he can field.

It really isn't a hindrance, and maybe because he's been deaf for so long, you learn how to manage it. You learn how to deal with what's going on, because in the heat of the moment, the center fielder, or whoever, is not going to remember, *Oh, yeah, Curtis is deaf, and I can't yell at him*. He just deals with it, and it really doesn't make any difference on the field. If you can play, you can play, regardless of whether you can hear or not.

—*Troy Glaus,*
LOS ANGELES ANGELS TEAMMATE

Curtis is a great guy. Forget about baseball, he is a good person. I played against him in the minor leagues and in the Arizona Fall League, and that's where I had the opportunity to get to know him.

And then he had those magical few games when he was my teammate on the Yankees. With what he has been through, what he's able to play with, it's amazing. Curtis Pride should be an inspiration to everyone.

—*Derek Jeter,*
New York Yankees teammate

You can forget Curtis is deaf. I was riding in his car with him one day, and usually when you're in a car, there's music on and you hear things, immediately there is some sort of station or a CD playing or something. But in his car it's completely silent.

I think he can feel the excitement. There are things he must deal with because he can't hear the other outfielders, more detailed things. I can't speak for him, but I really got a sense that he could feel the excitement and emotion, even though he can't hear it.

You wouldn't know he had a hearing disability, except for when you tried to notice it (compensate for it) or tried to speak slow. Speak in a normal dialect, face him, and he can read your lips.

—*Jason Varitek,*
Boston Red Sox teammate

Curtis Pride was somewhat of a hero to me. I often would talk to my coaches about Curtis and how he could instantly read balls off the bat and do different things in the outfield, considering the fact that all he had to tune himself into was watching the batter swing at the ball. I'd say to my coaches, "Do this," and push your ears completely closed where you can't hear anything and then go out and try to do what this guy does.

He had a lot of skills. I mean this guy could really run. He could absolutely fly. Until he was moved to Triple-A, he hit in the top of our order. It was like having a left-handed–hitting Rickey Henderson in the minor leagues, from the standpoint if you made a bad pitch to him, he's hitting a home run. An unbelievable sense of awareness on the bases. A great understanding of how and when to run from first to third. The visual perception that he had, because now as a base runner he can't hear the ball come off his teammates' bat, either. And knowing when to go from first to third, reading the body language of the outfielders and the angles that the outfielders were taking and realizing the fact that he could make it easily to third. All those kinds of things.

Anytime we needed a base runner, and he wasn't swinging the bat that well, he'd drop a bunt down. Anytime he made it a footrace between him and a pitcher or involved a first baseman and a pitcher on a fielding play, he was safe every time.

He was great with the other players. They would tease him and cut up with him good-naturedly. Just like he was one of the guys. He would laugh with them.

I was always very satisfied and pleased with the progress Curtis was making as a player. He constantly asked me questions, baserunning questions, fielding questions, offensive questions, should I have run there? This kid was a big-time student of the game and starving to learn everything that he could. I wasn't the least bit shy about openly talking to him about it. I felt that was part of my job as a minor-league manager. When he was wrong and I disagreed with him, I would tell him.

We had a very special team in Harrisburg that year, and Curtis was a huge part of it. If you were to map out the importance of teamwork, and what you can accomplish playing together as a team, that team, in my opinion, was the epitome of all of that. Because not only was it extremely talented, the players genuinely liked one another, they cared about one another, they played together, and they also played within the framework of each one of their individual abilities. They were unbeatable. You know something, when you're fifty games over .500 during the regular season, win the Eastern League Championship, and the final number with playoff victories is one hundred wins and only forty-seven losses, that's a pretty special baseball team.

Number one, it made you really appreciate what skills Curtis Pride had, but it also made you realize this person you're dealing with is a very special guy. This is a young man who is very committed to succeeding, when a lot of people are saying, due to his disability, we don't think he can. Yes, I was challenged by that. I knew this kid was committed to proving them wrong. I was challenged and committed to helping Curtis convince them, *yeah, you were wrong*, he did make it!

—*Jim Tracy*,
Double-A manager in Harrisburg, Pennsylvania

I'm not a stat guy. When you're talking about Curtis Pride, this is a champion among champions. The things that he has had to deal with, the things he has had to overcome, the things he has given back to society, not only in sports, but in life in general. I can't say enough about it.

The thing about Curtis is that he worked as hard as anybody ever has. He played as hard as anybody ever has. Curtis Pride was blessed—maybe it's because of his last name—but he was blessed with a great deal of pride. I loved having him on my team. This guy came to play every day. It was not just the will to win that was important to him, it was the will to prepare to win.

—*Steve Swisher*,
manager at Double-A Binghamton, New York

The first time I saw Curtis Pride, he was probably about ten years old. He was playing soccer against my son's team. Before the game even started, the kids were doing drills, and there was this little kid with a hearing aid running like the wind. It was just incredible. It was obvious to me right then that he was going to be a great athlete in something.

I think his deafness is all blown out of proportion, because I certainly never noticed any lack of ability in him to track the baseball. I think it's mostly sight and the line of the pitch and seeing the ball come off the bat, more than it is sound. If you've got fifty thousand people in the stands, yelling, and screaming, a lot of the time you don't even hear it.

He played center field on our high school team, but he could have played shortstop, probably could have pitched, could have played anywhere. Center and left center, and right center were all his.

The first thing I'd tell the pro scouts that came to our games was, first, he's a great person. Forget baseball, forget all the other sports, Curtis Pride is a great individual. He is one of the nicest kids and best citizens I've ever coached.

He played soccer, baseball, and basketball. I also coached football, and I saw him playing wide receiver once in a nontackle pickup game. As strong as he was naturally, he would have been a great running back. Nobody would have been able to catch him. I talked to his father one time and said, "Mr. Pride, would you consider Curtis playing football?" He said, "No." That was it. I never approached him again. John Pride is also a strong individual of great character.

The kids who played with him looked up to Curtis, even when he was a junior. It was a great ride for me. I really enjoyed coaching our practices and watching him develop.

Everybody has a dream, but of all the people I saw in my coaching career—thirty-three years in Montgomery County, Maryland—he was the one individual that I saw had the tools and the work habits to play far beyond high school and go as far as he wanted to go.

—*Ken Rippetoe,*
BASEBALL COACH AT KENNEDY HIGH SCHOOL

Curtis fit right in; he was no different than any other player on the team. He got great jumps on the ball. Some of the stadiums are so loud you can't hear the ball hit the bat. Curtis could anticipate it and he never had a problem picking up the ball off the bat. He was a great base runner. He would get great jumps because he had that extra instinct.

I remember it (his first major-league hit) very vividly. It was one of the most poignant moments of my career. Let me replay it for you.

We're playing the Phillies, and Curtis came in as a pinch hitter. We were in a big-time pennant race. There was a big crowd, an enormous one. Curtis hits a double at a crucial turning point in the game. After he hit the double, the fans were giving him a standing ovation and cheering him very loudly. What made such a big impact is the fact that the Phillies changed pitchers right after that hit, so there was a lot of time in between. During that time, as the third-base coach, I was able to go out to him and tell him that they wanted him to tip his cap. Curtis can read lips extremely well.

After he tipped his hat, he looked around and could see everybody. Players were very cognizant of what was going on at that time. They knew that this was a special moment where someone had beaten all the odds, and it came at a time in an important game when we really needed it.

He asked me, "Can I steal third?" I said, "No, no, that's not why I'm calling you over here. I'm calling you over because they're cheering, and they want you to tip your cap."

As I recollect, after the game, I asked him, "Did you hear that?"

He said, "No, but I could feel it in my chest." That was truly a very moving experience. Not only for myself, but for the entire team.

If they had one of those things where they measure the decibel level, it would have been off the chart, because it was almost as if they were trying to make him hear. You understand what I'm saying? They're trying to make him hear. They knew he couldn't, but they were going to the next level to do everything they could to make him hear.

What happened was, he felt it, which was probably as rewarding for him as it was for us to hear it.

—*Jerry Manuel,*
Montreal Expos third-base coach

Of all the players I signed to professional baseball contracts, Curtis Pride was the greatest signing I ever made. That one meant the most to me. It was the most interesting and the most rewarding contract I've ever done. I knew he had the ability to handle adversity. He had stared adversity down repeatedly.

Curtis was such a great kid, and he overcame so much, just in the game of baseball. So many people were saying he couldn't do it, but I knew he could handle the adversity. His attention to detail was off the charts. I made a lot of phone calls when I was scouting him in high school, and it was obvious he was a high-character kid. There were so many pluses, it added up that he could play at the big-league level. Not just a minor leaguer filling out a roster, but someone who could be a quality major-league player for a long time.

—*Carmen Fusco,*
New York Mets scout

The first time we met was in our English class, probably one of the first periods of the day in the school year. I don't know how it happened, but I was at his table. I was at Curtis's table, and I was asked to take notes for him, on this special paper, like duplicate paper so he could have my notes without having to make copies or run duplicates of them.

I played baseball. I had always been playing something, every fall—baseball in the spring, soccer in the fall. I was always involved in sports. I was okay. So Curtis and I had baseball in common. I was not a big basketball player. Baseball and golf became my sports. We played a lot of baseball together.

Our freshman year of high school, Curtis made the varsity team, and I made the junior varsity. During sophomore year I also made the varsity. Sometime in between there, we also joined a summer league together.

Through sports—we both enjoyed sports—he was obviously a lot more athletic than I was, but I was athletic, too, and did a lot of things. If I recall correctly, I helped him get into golf. I don't think he had played golf until I introduced him to it. I started playing when I was twelve or thirteen. I think he picked it up sometime when we were in high school.

I do remember through high school that not everyone embraced him. When near the end of high school and scouts were at all our baseball games, I sensed that some of our classmates got jealous of his abilities and all the attention he was getting. But those petty jealousies are probably pretty common with kids that age.

Curtis Pride is a great guy, and I am happy to know him as my lifelong friend.

—*Steve Grupe,*
BEST FRIEND

Curtis is very easy to communicate with. I think he works harder than the person communicating with him, so the burden is on Curtis. He goes above and beyond to make it easy for people to communicate with him. He reads lips, and communication was not an issue at all.

He's adapted, as most people do, to a weakness or a strength, whatever it might be. He's become adept—because he can't hear the sound of the ball off the bat—to what outfielders should do, which is swing planes, balance of the hitter, trajectory of the ball. There are a lot of things an outfielder will use to gauge the distance of the ball and he became more in tune with that because he wasn't able to have the audio.

There are certain guys in the clubhouse who have a presence and Curtis does. He's very intelligent, he knows the game, and he's a good person with a great understanding of baseball.

Curtis is a great guy, but he was here because he had a role to help us win. Curtis never wanted to be known as a ballplayer that had a hearing disability; he just wanted to be known as a good ballplayer.

—*Mike Scioscia,*
LOS ANGELES ANGELS MANAGER

Curtis always fit in like every other player and that's because of his upbringing. His parents deserve credit for much of his success, as they did everything they could to make sure he is probably among the top five percent in the entire world at reading lips. He played basketball at William & Mary, and he was able to do a lot of things because his parents brought him up to live in the regular world and not use his hearing disability as either an excuse or a privilege, which is remarkable.

I had him on a Winter League team in Venezuela, and there were a whole lot of things that were different. The first day he came to Venezuela was a Saturday night, and we had a Sunday game at 11:00 a.m. the next day. This was in 1994. One of our drivers picked him up at the airport and our Saturday night game was just finishing when he arrived at the stadium.

He had never played in Venezuela before. He had played a little bit in the big leagues the year before, not too much. Curtis was basically a minor-league player going down there, forced to learn about a new country, and everything that involves.

I knew him because he had played against me when he was with the St. Lucie Mets and then we acquired him, and he played with me as a coach, manager, and instructor.

That night, in Venezuela, I said, "We have an eleven a.m. game tomorrow, so you have to get up early." There was a time change to deal with, too.

I said, "How do you get up?"

He replied, "I have an alarm clock."

"Wait a minute. You have an alarm clock?" I asked him.

He answered, "Yeah, it shakes the bed, but I forgot to bring it."

"Don't worry, I'm staying at the same hotel. I'll call you," I assured him. Then it hit me: He wouldn't be able to hear the phone ring. But with Curtis, you'd often forget that he was deaf.

I took his room key and said, "I'll come by your room and wake you up." But then the next morning, I'm thinking about it as I am walking down to his room and thought, *Wait a second: Here's a man that is young and strong, and I'm going to go into his room while he's asleep and start shaking him! I'm going to get killed.* But sure enough, when I entered the room, he was already up and taking a shower, so I didn't have to worry.

Curtis wants to be treated like everyone else, but he also knows where he is. He knows how blessed he has been.

In West Palm Beach we had to play a tripleheader one night because we had a doubleheader scheduled the previous day, and the second game had been stopped by rain in the second inning. In A-ball, you pick it up in the second inning. The next night we picked up a game in the second inning, played the second game of the doubleheader, and then had the third game. Sure enough, the third game didn't even start until around midnight. We were in West Palm Beach, playing St. Lucie, and Curtis Pride was playing left field for them.

We had a kid named Fletcher playing second base and Pride was the runner on first base. There's a ground ball at 12:10 a.m., and Curtis Pride breaks up the double play and crushes Fletcher. But it was a legitimate slide, hard play. But it's 12:10 a.m., the third game of a tripleheader, and a ground ball in A-ball—and this guy is still giving it 100 percent effort, barreling in, legally, over our second baseman to play the game hard, the right way.

Felipe Alou and I looked at each other, and I said, "Boy, if we could ever get this guy, this is the kind of player you want on your team."

—*Dave Jauss,*
Montreal Expos coach,
manager in Venezuelan Winter League

Curtis had the ability to communicate all along, regardless of his impairment. He was just another one of the guys, really. Baseball is a funny thing. A lot of us have had handicaps, but in Curtis's case, he had a major impairment, because sound is something you really rely on at times in baseball. I expected it to be more of a challenge, but he always made it easy. It was never an issue.

In Curtis's case he learned how to live with it, how to deal with it, and became successful, regardless of his issues.

I always thought Curtis had the ability. In this game it's all about timing, too: being at the right place at the right time. Curtis Pride always worked hard and he made a nice career for himself.

—Buddy Bell,
Detroit Tigers manager

"Pride had the home run ball and the lineup card in his locker, souvenirs from his memorable first game as a Yankee. The rest of us had a reminder of human possibility, and of the great and noble honor in never giving up on a dream . . .

"Pride spoke of the honor of wearing the Yankee pinstripes and playing with Derek Jeter and Roger Clemens and so many other superstars, which made one thing odd yesterday. He seemed oblivious to just how much his new teammates should be honored to be playing with him."

—Lawrence Rocca,
Newark Star-Ledger sportswriter

"Now Curtis Pride had hit a home run as a Yankee at Yankee Stadium in front of 55,000, and Joe Torre and Don Zimmer were pushing him up the dugout steps and into a curtain call. Pride—born with inoperable nerve deafness—was asked how much he heard of the next moment, at the top of the dugout steps, how much he felt. 'I could feel Yankee Stadium vibrating,' Pride said. 'Vibrating all around me.'

"Curtis Pride did not hear all that we heard. He still got the better of the day. We did not feel what he felt."

—Mike Lupica,
New York Daily News columnist

Acknowledgments

Curtis Pride Acknowledgments

There are countless people I would like to thank for their role shaping my life and helping me realize my dreams.

First of all, I want to express my deepest appreciation to the two most important people in my life: My parents, John & Sallie Pride.

My mom and dad have made me the person that I am today by instilling a firm belief that anything is possible, a never-give-up attitude, and a strong work ethic. Thank you Mom and Dad for your guidance, wisdom, encouragement, support and, most importantly, your love. My sisters, Jacqui and Christine, also always had my back and looked out for me during our childhood, and I really appreciate everything they have done for me.

I would also like to thank my wife, Lisa, and my two children, Noelle and Colten, for their constant support and love. They are the center of my world and without them in my life, everything else would seem insignificant.

This book would not have been published without the unwavering persistence and commitment of my longtime agent, Joe Strasser. Joe has done so much for me and my family for the past thirty years that he has become much more than an agent. Joe is a true friend, a confidant, and more importantly, I truly feel like he is a part of my family. Joe and I have been through a lot together throughout both my career and personal life, and I can't thank him enough for standing by me, encouraging me, and believing in me.

A big thank you to Doug Ward, my writing collaborator on this book. When I decided to share my story in a memoir, I was very thorough in my process for selecting a writer to work with. Specifically, I wanted to collaborate with someone who I felt would devote the necessary time and effort to thoroughly understand everything I went through to achieve my dream of playing in the Major Leagues. Now that this book has been published, I know that I made the right choice. Doug, you did a terrific job, and it was a pleasure to work with you.

A bittersweet thank you to one of my closest family friends, Rick Barsky, who passed away before he could share in this book being published. I knew Rick since I was in high school when I used to take care of his yard. I want to thank Rick for all he did for me: he was my accountant, one of my lifelong supporters, and helped start this book project. I know he would be proud of how this book came out.

My sincere thanks go to a group of great coaches who have been extremely patient, supportive, encouraging and positive throughout my childhood baseball: T-ball coach Don Stein, Travel ball coach Jim Corsetty, Travel ball coach Wayne Nail, American Legion coach Herb Rutledge, Kennedy High School coach Buck Jones (my freshman year), and Kennedy High School coach Ken Rippetoe (my last three years of high school). A special shout out to Coach Rippetoe who generously worked out with me many times to improve my baseball skills, and for giving me a key to the Kennedy HS training facility so I could take batting practice on my own.

At William & Mary, Dr. Carroll Hardy, dean of students for multicultural affairs and special needs, was a great advocate. Dean Hardy has since passed away, but my gratitude for her interest and guidance in my academic career will live within me forever.

I would like to acknowledge two New York Mets scouts who signed me to my first professional contract: Scout Bob Dawson and his scouting supervisor, Carmen Fusco. There is a saying in professional baseball that a player never forgets and fondly remembers the scout who scouted and signed him to his first professional contract.

That is very true for me and Carmen Fusco. Carmen, thank you for believing in me when I was just a young guy in high school and starting me on my path to the major leagues.

I also would like to acknowledge Roland Johnson, the Mets Scouting Director, for drafting me and working out a deal with my parents to allow me to be a full-time college student/basketball player and a part-time minor-league baseball player every year for four years until graduation.

In the minor leagues, I was very fortunate and blessed to stay with wonderful families whose generosity I will never forget: Vernon and Teresa Smith (Kingsport, TN), Lucille Reilly and Jeannie Ortega (Pittsfield, MA), Buzz and Flo Mathis and two sons (Columbia, SC), Phillip and Rose Grady (Binghamton, NY) and Phillip and Diane Anido and their three kids (Ottawa, Canada).

I would like to specifically thank two minor-league coaches in particular who played a significant role in my climb to the Majors: Steve Swisher (Binghamton Mets) and Jim Tracy (Harrisburg Senators).

I would like to thank my closest friends who have been my side throughout my life: Randy Hurowitz (longtime childhood friend/ neighbor who recently passed away), Steve Grupe (best friend since high school), Sean Hughes (high school friend/soccer teammate), Jon Gregory (high school friend/basketball teammate), Eric Rosenberg (high school friend/soccer teammate), Kenny Bloom, (high school friend and college roommate), Thierry Chaney (college friend), Vince Edwards (college friend), Dick Tracey (college friend/college roommate). Many other people—far too many to list here—have played an important role in my life. To those friends and family members, you know who you are, and you know how much you mean to me.

Special thanks to Cal Ripken Jr. for writing the book's foreword and for providing an ideal role model for how to play the game.

Finally, but importantly, I would like to thank Kensington Publishing and specifically editor Leticia Gomez and her entire team for patiently guiding the manuscript through the editing and production process to produce an inspirational book of which I am extremely proud.

—*Curtis Pride*

Doug Ward Acknowledgments

I will be forever grateful to Curtis Pride for trusting me to tell his remarkable life story. Curtis was an ideal collaborator, bringing me into his world, candidly opening his heart and giving generously of his time to co-write this book.

Curtis's parents, John & Sallie Pride, invited me into their home, spending countless hours sharing precious memories as they poured through photo albums and mementos while recounting how they raised Curtis and their two daughters, Christine and Jacqui.

Joe Strasser, Curtis's agent, was relentless in his determination to get this story out into the world and was a go-to source for anything related to Curtis's baseball career. Were it not for Joe's unwavering belief in the importance of Curtis's story, you would not be reading these words now.

Thanks to the many interview subjects who gave freely of their time to share recollections of Curtis, among them Jim Tracy, Jerry Manuel, Steve Swisher, and Mike Quade. Steve Grupe was always receptive to revisiting the early days of his lifelong friendship with Curtis, as was Rick Barsky, who sadly did not live to see the book's publication.

Special thanks to Cal Ripken Jr. for writing the book's foreword, and to John Maroon for his professionalism. Thanks to Jeff Moeller, who read an early draft of the manuscript and provided insightful feedback. Eric Waldhaus and Phyllis Pacifico also read early drafts and provided helpful notes.

The skilled editing and kindness of Leticia Gomez at Kensington Publishing took this book to new heights as she deftly guided first-time authors through the publishing process. I am appreciative of the entire team at Kensington who worked tirelessly to elevate this title, including production editor Robin Cook, designer Seth Lerner who created a compelling cover design, and Stephanie Finnegan for her meticulous copy editing. I would be remiss if I did not express my appreciation and admiration for the publicity and marketing savvy of Vida Engstrand and Michele Addo-Chajet, whose belief in this book never wavered.

I am indebted to Leslie Kallen for her unwavering belief, dedication and friendship, and to the endlessly supportive Richard Walter, a great writer and inspirational teacher.

Most of all, my love and gratitude goes to my wife, Heather, a constant source of positivity, who read multiple drafts of the manuscript, always offering insightful notes, along with encouragement and support.

—Doug Ward

AFTERWORD

John Lewis Pride

1940–2024

It is with a heavy heart that I write this tribute to my father, John, who passed away, September 22, 2024, during the production of this book. While he got to see and read the entire manuscript during the editing process, my dad was also looking forward to seeing the fully published book. But he already knew the story better than anyone because he was with me every step of the way and his imprint is on every page. Along with my mom Sallie, my dad played a huge role in my upbringing and helped shape me into the man I am today.

My dad was extremely proud of me and loved to brag to both friends and strangers about my accomplishments. But here's the thing: I am even more proud of my dad for the type of person he was, the values he championed throughout his life, and the way he treated everyone he met with respect. This is my turn to brag to the world about what kind of man John Pride was.

When I was eight years old, I learned an early lesson about my dad's character when he took me to an indoor swimming center in Rockville, Maryland. I was so excited about spending time with my dad in the pool while he taught me how to swim. That day at the pool, however, I was disappointed when my father asked another volunteer to teach me to swim. During the ride home afterward, I asked my dad why he didn't spend any time with me in the pool. His answer summarized his lifelong commitment to service, telling me that he volunteered to help someone every week, someone who needed his help more than I did, someone less fortunate than we were. At the pool that day, my dad was helping a young girl named Cathy who had a severe form of cerebral palsy.

My dad told me there would be plenty of time for me and him to do all kinds of fun things together and, as always, he was true to his word. That day I understood the type of man my dad was—always giving his time to help those who needed it the most. The following week we went back to the pool and my dad helped Cathy again. That's when I noticed that Cathy was loving every minute of being in the pool with my dad—safe, secure, and happy—and it made me very proud that he was bringing a smile to her face, spending time with her in the pool every week.

He was a devoted family man who, along with his wife and my mother, Sallie, raised three children while also welcoming foster kids into their home. Not surprisingly, his professional life was dedicated to the service of others, as evidenced by a 35-year civil servant career with the federal government that spanned eight different presidential administrations. One of his work highlights was investigating the state's compliance with Title VI of the Civil Rights Act (desegregation) in the South, which led to the landmark Kerner Commission report under President Johnson. After he retired in 2003, he worked as the Executive Director of The National Practitioners Network for Fathers and Family and as a consultant monitoring Head Start program compliance across the country.

The quintessential man for all seasons, my dad was always current on the latest developments in sports or world events and ready to offer an insightful analysis that was somehow both nuanced and accessible. He was a foodie before the term existed, especially when it came to grilling pork ribs with Papa Pride's BBQ sauce (his special delicious homemade BBQ sauce), a voracious reader of books across all genres, and a veritable goodwill ambassador for the many benevolent organizations to which he volunteered his time and money freely, including The Capital University Alumni Association of which he was an extremely proud graduate, as well as a multitude that had a direct impact on my story, including: The Alexander Graham Bell Association for the Deaf and Hard of Hearing, the Montgomery

County Association for Hearing Impaired Children, Big Brothers, and the Boys and Girls Club. He particularly enjoyed coaching many baseball, softball, and basketball teams. Because of the indelible impact that he had on my family and other people, he was recognized by the National Urban League as one of the "Top 50 Fathers" in the Metro DC area in 1993.

If you were lucky enough to know him, you had a loyal friend, resolute advocate, and thoughtful advisor.

To me, John Lewis Pride was all of that and more.

—Curtis Pride